Nobody's Son

ALSO BY MARK SLOUKA

Brewster: A Novel

Essays from the Nick of Time

The Visible World

God's Fool

Lost Lake: Stories

*War of the Worlds: Cyberspace and
the High-tech Assault on Reality*

Nobody's Son

A Memoir

Mark Slouka

W. W. NORTON & COMPANY
Independent Publishers Since 1923
New York | London

For information about permission to reproduce selections from this book,
write to Permissions, W. W. Norton & Company, Inc.,
500 Fifth Avenue, New York, NY 10110

For information about special discounts for bulk purchases, please contact
W. W. Norton Special Sales at specialsales@wwnorton.com or 800-233-4830

Manufacturing by Quad Graphics, Fairfield
Book design by Ellen Cipriano
Production manager: Louise Mattarelliano

Library of Congress Cataloging-in-Publication Data

Names: Slouka, Mark, author.
Title: Nobody's son : a memoir / Mark Slouka.
Description: First edition. | New York : W. W. Norton & Company, 2016.
Identifiers: LCCN 2016018257 | ISBN 9780393292305 (hardcover)
Subjects: LCSH: Slouka, Mark—Family. | Slouka, Mark—Childhood and
youth. | Czech Americans—Biography. | Authors, American—
Biography. | Mothers and sons—New York (State)—Biography. | Family
secrets—New York (State). | New York (State)—Biography.
Classification: LCC PS3569.L697 Z46 2016 | DDC 813.54 [B] —dc23 LC
record available at https://lccn.loc.gov/2016018257

W. W. Norton & Company, Inc.
500 Fifth Avenue, New York, N.Y. 10110
www.wwnorton.com

W. W. Norton & Company Ltd.
15 Carlisle Street, London W1D 3BS

1 2 3 4 5 6 7 8 9 0

FOR YOU, BACK WHEN.

Each one wraps himself in what burns him.

DANTE

I

IN THE SUMMER OF 1970, when I was twelve years old, my mother and father and I spent three months in a big wooden house on the shore of one of the Twin Lakes in the northwestern corner of Connecticut. My father, a professor of political science, had gotten a summer teaching gig at some institute of international something-or-other. It came with a house, so up we went.

There may be more beautiful places on earth than northwestern Connecticut in the summer, but if there are, I haven't seen them yet. I remember that house, that place—the creaky wooden steps, the well-balanced cedar doors, the click of the tongue in the latch. I remember the track of moonlight across the lake, the rain hissing in the long grass at noon. I fell in love that summer. Her name was Karen. She and her brother, Kevin, were adopted. Their stepsister, Laura, liked me, but I loved Karen. Karen had long blond hair and, if memory serves, ever-so-slightly crossed eyes, and I loved her. How she felt about me didn't really come up. Bread's "I Wanna Make It with You" was on the radio that summer, as was Freda Payne's "Band of Gold." Those songs were about us. Every song was about us.

Sitting here by the open window forty-four years later, the songs playing that summer are still about us, though time has erased her face, her voice. Such is the adhesive property of memory, which can cling to a song, God help us, for as long as memory serves.

One hot night in July or August the students and faculty threw a party at another house on the shore of the lake. There was a barefoot crowd and the smell of burning meat and cut grass and someone had carried the stereo out on the wide, creaky porch and was playing every Beatles record known to man, in order. My parents were somewhere in the crowd. That night Karen and Kevin and Laura and I swam in the dark with the college kids then waded along the shore strung with white paper lanterns, and at some point Karen bent over to pick something out of the water and I saw her breasts swaying like small, pale fruit inside the wet cave of her t-shirt. I don't remember if she saw that I'd seen. I'd like to think she did, that our eyes met for a long second, both of us aware of something just a few steps beyond us, and then I looked away and that was that. It doesn't matter.

The Beatles' "Blackbird" playing from the porch of that rambling, lit-up house. The "hippies" with their flowers and their hammocks who moved into the house next door to us. The day our friends, the Horners, drove up from Philadelphia to visit and I was allowed to show their boys my air rifle. The thousand ping-pong games in the institute's wooden rec room, the rain drumming on the tin roof—these were good things. There were many of them. Sundays I'd wake up early while everything was still cool and wet and full of summer and ride my bicycle out to a field where I'd pick a bouquet of black-eyed Susans—such a strange name for a flower—for my mother, who was going crazy.

We don't always remember what we deserve to, or want to. We remember what we have to, which isn't quite the same thing. We remember because one memory has elbowed aside the others.

A warm night, the heaviness of coming rain in the air. Sitting in the wide back seat of our car in the dark—was it the white Pontiac?—listening to them fight, I didn't think about it much at first. There'd been a lot of fights. Only a few had been really bad; most were just vicious, marked by a rage—my mother's mostly—distilled into something so pure it stung your eyes. Once when I was seven or eight, she'd locked herself in the bathroom of our little house in Ardsley and my father, worried that she'd "do something," tried to force the door open. I remember him straining like a rugby player, shoulder to the wood. I'd been in my room reading *Field and Stream*—I remember this for some reason—a special section they had then called "Tap's Tips," in which someone named Tappy offered tips on knots and baits and how to solve problems like backlash on your bait casting reel, but at some point, hearing the door slam, then slam again, I came out. Mommy was screaming, though when I summon that sound now, and it comes back surprisingly easily, I see the word isn't quite right. Screaming implies terror, but this wasn't the sound of someone trying to save themselves from a killer, this was the sound of someone outraged enough to kill. When my father managed to reach into the bathroom, my mother grabbed his hand and raked her nails down the length of his forearm. "Look at this," he said, holding out his arm to me, the four welling furrows, the skin accordioned half an inch high at the end of each row. "Look at what she's done!"

Amazing, really, what time, or ego, can force into being. What we learn to own. A few months before my father died in Prague in 2012—I didn't know there was so little time left then—I noticed the shadows, long and light as sheet scars, on his forearm, and felt a touch of ownership. I'd been there when they were made.

What I'm saying is that there had been other times. More than a few. This time in the car was different.

They were arguing about the end-of-the-session party we were returning from, about some nineteen-year-old ingenue who'd apparently been flattering my father, holding his big square hand in hers and telling him how very, very much his course had meant to her—no, really, so much more than she could say in words. My mother, who no one ever accused of being a fool, was more outraged, I think, by my father's gullibility than anything else. He was a stuttering idiot, a laughingstock. "It means so much to me," she mimicked like a girl trapped in some dark fairy tale, changing into something bad. "It means more than I can say in words."

It didn't stop. My father, who I hardly remember saying a thing, sat there like a rock as her rage built on itself, fed off itself, until it had left the original goad far behind. It was just rage now. I remember yelling at them to stop, just stop, but by then she'd started hitting him with her fists, hitting him as if he really were that rock and she was determined to smash him into something . . . other. Or maybe nothing at all.

I was probably crying by then—it wouldn't surprise me— though I don't remember. They'd forgotten I was there. We were on the mile-long dirt road that led to our house, and my father was still driving, flinching, his right shoulder hunched up against her fists. When she snuck one around and smashed his professor's horn-rimmed glasses off his face he had to stop, and that's when I ran.

I didn't know I was going to run. I had nowhere to go. I just opened the back door and ran, my hands up against the branches, and the woods closed around me.

I remember sitting quietly with my back against a pine tree, listening to them stumble around in the woods, calling me. Worried now, pleading with me to come out. They didn't have a flashlight. There was no moon. I'd disappeared. "Where on earth has he gone?" I remember my mother saying. It was my mother's voice again.

I could see our car, lit up like a small room in the dark, its doors open. I didn't answer for a while. I could hear the fear in their voices, and it troubled me. Eventually I came out. Where else was I going to go? It had always been the three of us. Maybe my mother offered to make me my favorite breakfast—jam-filled Czech crepes called *palačinky*. Maybe one of them made a joke. Probably they spoke to the dark about how mommies and daddies sometimes fight and it doesn't really mean anything and so on. I came out. I loved them.

I'd know better now. I've been hunting for that place—so lonely, so sheltering, so free of their pain—for a long time. If I found it now—and I don't know that I've ever needed it more— I'd stay in the dark and smile. Let them blunder off into the night.

It's your turn to be afraid now, I'd think.

II

WHO KNOWS WHERE WE come from, really? We tell stories to explain us, but like all origin myths ours is retrospective, a fiction cobbled together to validate who we are—to justify what is, or excuse it. So very logical. After a while you believe it yourself. And then the divining rod dips and you sense another source.

All my life, the woods have been my sanctuary. I thought it was just love. In fifth and sixth and seventh grade at Pocantico Hills Central School in Tarrytown, New York, where my mother was the school librarian, I'd engineer elaborate escapes, stringing together two, three, four school periods during which one teacher would think I was with another, and run. I can still remember the thrill of pulling on the clay-colored sweatshirt and ratty pair of sneakers I kept hidden in a garbage bag in the weeds (or buried in the snow) behind the equipment shed so that I wouldn't get my school clothes muddy, wriggling on my back under the wires, vanishing into the trees. These were the Rockefeller estate's woods, 3,500 acres of overgrown roads and deserted forests and lakes with dark fringes of pine where the great horned owls nested in the spring, vomiting up their little marbles of hair and bone for me to find on the shelves of late-season snow.

I lived there, dreamed of returning when I was gone. I wrote ten-year-olds' stories about disappearing into the woods, vanishing. Even as a young man, college-age and older, I had a strange, atavistic fantasy of escaping into some equatorial rain forest, reverting, forgetting. This wasn't erasure, it was fulfillment. I could see myself squatting naked in the dark with a bloody stick in my hand, the alluvial mud rising in soft fronds between my toes, more animal than human now, unspeakably alive.

The natural world has been my religion, which makes sense; what has religion ever been but a refuge from the things that frighten us? But I wonder now if what I thought was innate was actually made, if one home's collapse didn't force another into being. If my mother and father, pointing out a milk snake disappearing into the foundation of our cabin, or a stick insect clinging to the screen, weren't instilling this love, recognizing, in some unadmitted way, that it would make as good a haven from them as any.

III

THERE CAN COME A time in your life when the past decides to run you down. You're not going to get away. Take the hit.

I thought I'd gotten away. I'd written about the past for twenty years. I'd told the story, bent by fiction like an oar in water, over and over, inoculating myself. I thought it was enough. It wasn't.

"And so they are ever returning to us, the dead," the writer W.S. Sebald wrote. Yes, well. Define "dead."

In the spring of 2014 the invisible world decided to put in an appearance. I couldn't move, couldn't laugh, couldn't write. I didn't know what was happening. The novel I was writing kept twisting like a heliotrope toward betrayals I'd never intended my characters to feel. I'd always been a mad dreamer: burial and resurrection, thousand-foot waves. My dreams now were relentless, exhausting, obvious as a club. In one I had to bury our dog, and my father, who'd died the year before, appeared to help me. It was night, and we went out into the dark and I put my hand on his damp shirt-back and the coolness of his sweat felt so familiar that I realized it was him I had to bury, that he was there to make it easier for me. In another, a pathetic old woman, so thin you could see the blue skeleton moving under her skin like a second self, sat slumped against a brick wall. When I reached out to help her she gripped my arm with the strength of a hydraulic press. She started to push the silver penknife I keep on my desk into my eye, then forced it into my mouth instead. I was struggling, trying to keep my tongue to the flat of the tiny blade when I woke up.

There were others, night after night, week after week, like knuckles rapping on a wooden door. It felt like a beating. It also felt ridiculous, an *Onion* headline: "Man Beats Himself Bloody, Files Suit." I could see my wife and daughter, who know me well, who know my resilience, watching from the sidelines, trying to help. When our son called from Peru, he asked me how I was doing and I said I was fine. He sounded worried, which wasn't like him.

I was drinking more than necessary, nothing Fitzgerald-esque, just nice and steady. It didn't help. When I went for a run, it was to experience a pain I could understand. I flailed and floundered. The things that had always given me pleasure—the fly rod in the evenings, music, good books and so-so movies—were losing their power. Sex still helped, but sex as an escape, though better than heroin, is about as likely to cure what ails you.

It had been a little over a year since my father died. I missed him terribly: his big, damp forehead, his voice, his being in the world. My mother, who I'd once loved unreservedly, whose voice had been like a second soul to me, was in a care home in Moravia, her mind having long ago lost any trace of me. I hadn't seen her in three years.

It took a while for me to begin to crack it. In 2013, not long after my father had died, I'd written a piece for *The New Yorker* called "Nobody's Son." I'd liked the title at the time; only now did I see that like one of those overpriced Russian nesting dolls you buy on impulse then regret for years, it had a deeper core: the desire to be done, to begin again, to wipe the tabula rasa. My father was gone, my mother's memory—of me and everything else—gone as well and not coming back. Time to pee on the fire and go.

As if it could ever be that simple. As if our words could ever have that much power. As if simply calling something a New World could make it one. No, if history had taught me anything, it was that ghosts tended to hang around, insisting on their place at the table, disturbing the atmosphere, clinking their glasses for another toast—an ironic one.

Nobody's son? I was pinned like Ahab to his whale. In the spring of 2014, the man my mother had met after leaving my father had passed away. I didn't miss him, one of those small, angry souls always hoarding their grievances, waiting for an opportunity to bite. The problem was, there was no one else. Just me. I'd quit, cleaned out my desk, handed in the keys. Now I had to be somebody's son again.

I had no choice—she was my mother. Almost overnight, stories, memories, the names of people I hadn't thought about in years, welled up like groundwater from some overfilled aquifer. I couldn't believe it—it seemed too obvious, a psychoanalytic cliché. Somehow my mother's story was flooding mine, or, more accurately, erasing it. I was reminded of the *Back to the Future* movies, Michael J. Fox's image fading out of the photograph, the stone wall showing through his jeans. If this was the return of the repressed, it was coming home in a tank.

Go ahead, my subconscious seemed to be saying. You want to shed all that messy history? You want to strike out like the American Adam with your freeze-dried beef stroganoff and your telescoping walking stick? You want to fucking baptize yourself? Well good luck and God bless—I'll drown you like a cat in a well.

If freedom was my goal, it wouldn't be achieved through magical thinking; a little blood was required.

I'd have to write my way back into being.

This much I knew—it wouldn't be easy. I'd never allowed myself to write about them. Us. Not directly. I'd hidden the three of us in fiction, story after story, book after book. I'd told the truth but I told it slant. Was it decency or cowardice? All my life I've been better at taking pain than giving it, which suggests a bit of both.

There's more. I think—and this is embarrassing—that I was embarrassed, afraid of seeming . . . what? Self-pitying? Self-indulgent? Soft? All of the above? This wasn't just the curse of the American male, hard-wired to suck it up, gut it out, shrug and smile. I didn't want to be the whiner, the one flogging his finger's worth of first-generation unhappiness into tragedy. The daily paper bulged with heartbreak, with stories of ordinary people bearing more than you could imagine if you allowed yourself to try. What possible excuse could I have for wading into this lake, adding my cupful?

Not that I wouldn't talk to you about our family—I would. I

believed in the magic of articulating what ails you, exorcism without the bullshit.

Talk, talk, talk. Man, but I could talk. I'd talk to you till the
cows came home and left again. Thirty years of professing at six
different universities will do that to you. Dante to Dickinson, Melville to Musil, I knew about orphans and exile, immigration and
war, original sin and the ways of memory. The unspeakable rich-
ness of this life, the tales we tell others and ourselves, were my
bread and butter. How many nights had I sat up late over that third
glass of wine happily untangling the world like a snarled fishing
reel, rejoicing in its complexity.

Of all the fools in the world, the ones hiding behind their
self-awareness may be the worst. You can know yourself, or think
you do, and be none the wiser, analyze your predicament to the nth
degree and be no closer to escaping it. Melville had put it beauti-
fully: "For in tremendous extremities human souls are like drowning men; well enough they know they are in peril; well enough
they know the cause of that peril;—nevertheless, the sea is the sea,
and these drowning men do drown."

I didn't know that then. My head was still above water. I'd
talk about the past—that long saga of love and betrayal, forever
shadowed by war—then undercut it. I had my pop-culture props:
The whistling crucifixion scene at the end of *The Life of Brian*
("Just look on the bright side of life"); the knight, laughing off
his amputated arm in *Monty Python and the Holy Grail*—"Bah! A
mere flesh-wound."

I'd tell you, for example, about the summer evening, straight
out of a Daubigny oil, when my mother and I sat by the side of a

black-water pond named Skalák in central Moravia. The still air smelled of hot fields and manure. I was seventeen, and she explained to me how she just wanted to die, then pulled a small, plastic vial out of her pocket and showed me how many pills it would take— because she'd figured it out—shaking them out into her hand. "I just want to sleep and not wake up," she said. I'd explain to you how I talked to her for two, three, four hours—and not just that evening but all through high school, because she couldn't get out of bed, because everything betrayed you, because "life was a death sentence"—arguing for this world like some acne-ridden lawyer way beyond his depth. I'd tell you the pills were green and white, that I used to make up excuses to wake her, just to be sure, and when it all got too heavy, I'd shrug. "Let me tell you about my mother," I'd smile, quoting the scene in *Blade Runner* in which the replicant, forced to answer one question too many, blows away his questioner. "Let me tell you about my mother"—except that instead of then pointing the imaginary gun at somebody else, I'd point it at my own head, and laugh.

I wasn't a liar. I wasn't even wrong—laughter can be as good a way of dealing with the things we can't deal with as any. I just wasn't listening.

———

So here I was. Years ago I'd thought of using a quote from Faulkner's *As I Lay Dying* as an epigraph to a novel called *Brewster*, then exchanged it for something else and forgot about it. It came back to me now like a rejected lover who gets the last laugh: "You see me now, don't you?"

I would think how words go straight up in a thin line, quick and harmless, and how terribly doing goes along the earth, clinging to it.

A hard line for a writer to credit, and like most beautiful lines, only half-true, but a line I needed to hear. Certain things had been done—in 1933 and 1945 and 1970—steps taken, blows struck, doors closed, and they had to be acknowledged. Condemned, redeemed, forgiven, but above all, acknowledged. "Each of us has his own way of emerging from the underground," Kafka wrote, though he didn't make it far—"mine is by writing."

Besides pictures and memories—the airiest fictions of all—words were all I had. But these would be different words—words as a form of listening.

IV

MAYBE GUILT IS THE secret heart of every immigrant's story, however desired or necessary the leaving may have been. Guilt over your betrayal, guilt for having abandoned the home you were born into, its sounds and tastes, the *feel* of that place, that past.

When immigrant parents die, the sense of betrayal is reduced to language and inherited by their children. Writing about my mother and father now, I have this inescapable sense that I'm lying because they were never mom and dad, but *maminka a tatínek*. Just saying the words aloud, how quickly they're resurrected— and me along with them. There we are. I was Denda, or, as a kid, Dendiček, the *ček* suffix doing the same cutesifying work as the Spanish *ito*, say, or the German *chen*. I had nicknames: Špuntík, or "little cork," and Šefík, "little boss," because I was a stocky, self-assured little beggar at three.

The lies begin with the language; you have to allow for it like a statistician calculating standard deviation. Calling for me in the woods that night in 1970, my mother didn't say, "Where on earth has he gone?" but, *Ježíš, Marie, kde je?* which translates to "Jesus, Mary, where is he?" To translate it that way, though, would have been wrong, a small violence against the moment, against the strange reservoir of strength she always tapped into in moments of crisis. It would have suggested a religiosity that wasn't there. "Jesus Christ, where is he?" on the other hand, would have risked introducing a hint of irritation, obscuring the "what have we done?" note in her voice. To get it right I had to lie.

Every immigrant's kid faces this dilemma, this sense of estrangement. If you spoke Spanish or German or French at home, *mommy*'s a word; *mamacita* or *Mutti* or *maman* is your mother suddenly calling you in for dinner. The same would be true, of course, if you grew up speaking English in Beijing. The words *mommy* and *daddy* would forever conjure Mommy and Daddy. The ones you knew. Who knew you.

Every now and then, when I was young, we'd run into immigrant families who cut the past like a rope. *Jenom anglicky!* Only English! Even then it seemed perverse to me, like willing yourself into amnesia. How do you make yourself forget? In the case of one kid, the old language died before the new one took root, leaving him stranded in a world I find hard to imagine. Eventually his new, English-speaking self took hold, yet I wonder if today, half a century later, he still sometimes dreams in Czech, and if he does, if he understands what his dreams are saying, or if the language he left behind is like the people we meet in dreams—people we've never known, who seem so terribly familiar.

In my family we stuck with Czech. I wouldn't trade it. It intensified our exile, our isolation—concentrated us, as in a reduction sauce—but it was who we were.

One time, my wife-to-be came out of my room in the old house in Bethlehem, Pennsylvania, where we'd gone to visit my parents, to find me sitting on the beige sofa in the living room, talking to my mother, tears of anger and frustration running down my face. It was her first visit—we'd just met.

She asked me about it later, and I tried to explain, but it was impossible. Let me tell you about my mother? In what language? How could I explain that Mommy had her ways and means, that she could break you. Whatever explaining there was to be done— of whatever love, or betrayal, whatever grief turning in on itself— had to be done in Czech. I'd run into the first, most obvious layer of exile: the problem of language, of the essence that refuses translation. Let me tell you about my mother? Maybe the replicant shot his questioner out of frustration.

There's nothing to be done—it just needs to be said. I still speak Czech. I dream in it often. But I live and write in English. I try to tell the truth. Sometimes I fail less badly than others.

The distortion, the deviation, are inevitable. It's like writing about childhood, a different form of exile.

It is what it is. Acknowledge it. Move on.

V

I NEED TO SAY this up front. This memoir—how uncomfortable that word still is for me—isn't a straight story. It's a nest of memories, a tangle of anecdotes, told to me and misheard, misremembered; of regrets and revisions forced by time; of days and words lying dormant, sometimes for decades, until something—some dream, some secret cue—cracked their husk to a small, provisional understanding. In short, it's complex, nonlinear, sometimes contradictory, often inconclusive—a bit of a mess. A lot like life, if I get it right.

It's like this because I believe the record of our time, told as truly as possible, is never, or rarely, chronological. Life is always looping back, revising itself, elaborating itself; it's constantly intersecting with others' lives, responding to new facts—or what appear to us as facts—being shaped by motivations barely understood that are themselves constantly evolving, or fading, or strenuously denying their own existence.

When it comes to memory, chronology isn't a lie; it's a wish-fulfillment fantasy, an attractive oversimplification, at best, a happy accident. All right—a lie.

Fiction is a different kind of lie—an inescapable one. The past tense, by which I mean all memory, all history, the story of what you did this morning, is the domain of fiction. Try as we may, we can't help but shape what was, any more than we can help shaping ourselves.

An example? In the opening section of this memoir I told the "story" of the summer my family and I spent up in northwest Connecticut when I was twelve. Embedded in that story was the day that our friends, the Horners, came to visit.

Objective truth? Well, we were friends with a family named Horner, who visited us the summer of 1970—and I have a fine memory of showing off my new air rifle to their boys—but I left out a few things. I left out that Mr. and Mrs. Horner had faded blue numbers tattooed on the white skin of their forearms, courtesy of Treblinka, as I recall. I left out that Mr. Horner, who was barely five feet tall and the walking definition of the word "mensch," claimed that he had no problem with his stature because it had saved his life, that on a death march near the end of the war, as German children coached by soldiers practiced their aim by shooting at the heads of those staggering past, his size had kept him hidden in the crowd.

Leaving these things out didn't make my story of that day untrue, it just shaped it—which is how it has to be if we're to tell anything at all.

The past? My God, sometimes I think it's the biggest fiction of all, that "was" is just a convenient way of separating two eternities that otherwise would overlap like transparencies on an overhead projector. If the dead are gone, why do I continue to talk to them, think of them, dream of them? If those words my father said, or didn't say, are done, if that shameful thing I did twenty years ago is over, why am I still compensating, denying the pain, striving for some balancing decency?

I don't believe in beginnings. I just don't. I know they're convenient to believe in, that like the idea of God they give a certain shape to our lives, that the New World was dreamed on that notion, but I just can't. The root always goes deeper. Always. Everything is a reaction—whether imitation or resistance—to something earlier, and if that makes us feel less original than we'd like, less self-made, it shouldn't. It's how we answer the shaping pressure of the past that makes us who we are.

The payoff, of course—the flip side of the emoticon frown— is that if beginnings don't exist, neither do endings.

I was born on a night of heavy snow in Queens, New York, in 1958, but the gears were already engaged, the Fates doing their thing. My mother, beautiful, still able to laugh, already carried around the image, the voice, of the man—the love of her life— whom she'd met the year she married my father. My father, his thinning, dark hair combed straight back and his rimless glasses giving him the look of an athlete standing for his final exams, had already watched Hitler's motorcade enter Brno, Czechoslovakia, run guns to partisans' barns in Moravia, shoveled coal in Chullora, Australia.

Everything was already in play when I dropped like a marble into the immigrants' wheel.

VI

I LOVED HER, YES, but the word falls short; for a time, for years, I *was* her. We hadn't separated yet—we were like a half-fissioned cell, still sharing a single nucleus. At night in our old apartment in Queens, she'd curl herself against my back and I'd smell her perfume, her hair, the deep, cave-like warmth of her, and she'd hum some Czech song or other until I pretended to be asleep. She loved me. We'd always lie on our right sides for some reason (only now do I realize it was because the left side of my bed was pushed against the wall, forcing her to climb in from the right), my head tucked under her chin and her left arm around me, and often—it's one of the things I remember about her most clearly—her fingers would twitch against my stomach or my chest as if she were playing the piano that she used to play as a little girl.

My wife tells me my own fingers twitch slightly when I'm falling asleep, though I've never played the piano in my life. A legacy I can live with.

It's not surprising that it took my mother so long to teach me to hate her, or that when I learned it at last, I embraced it like an apostate drowning his doubt.

The hate that replaces love is always a violent thing; to rip out those roots, you have to reach deep, get a good grip, close your eyes and pull. Ignore that strange loosening in your chest.

VII

IN THE PHOTOGRAPH—"CATSKILLS, KAZIMIRS', 1956??" my mother's written on the back—they sit side by side in Adirondack chairs half-buried in the uncut grass. It's summer—that deep, grateful shade. If you look closely, you can make out tiny planes of light in the tall, sweating glasses on the arms of their chairs—the ice cubes in their drinks forever unmelted.

I can feel it in the way they're sitting, in the afternoon breeze blurring the carnations behind my mother's left shoulder. My father's just said something to the person with the camera; my mother, wearing a short terrycloth robe over her bathing suit, is looking down, smiling, like she can't help it. Like they've just had an argument and she's still angry but she can't help it. They're happy.

This was true, too. Whatever came later, this was true.

How much easier it would be if, like the Manichaeans of old or yesterday's talk-show hosts, we could split the universe into darkness and light.

———————

For a time they loved each other, loved me. I know that. I do. It's the most difficult thing for me now. I can see it in the pictures—the two of them hovering over me as a newborn, tickling my belly, rejoicing in my senile, gassy smile. I can read it in the entry that my mother, propped up on pillows in her hospital bed, wrote in her diary the day I was born—an entry I didn't find until fifty-six years later, four years after she'd forgotten she'd ever had a son. "A little boy was born to us today. . . . "

I was their rivet for a while—maybe longer than I knew.

That I wasn't enough, that the wars, both civil and not, already threatening to tear us apart would have their say, doesn't take away from the fact that, for a while, everything held. In fact, it's a miracle it held as long as it did. I'd been born into a hurricane; those first years were the eye.

VIII

THEY SAY THE SOUL tempered by fire—tortured true—is the better for the trial. I'd have to say it depends on the soul. And the fire.

I'll never know what they went through. Not really. Or how I would have survived it myself. My experience was not theirs. I was born between the wars.

I'll never know. It hasn't stopped me from trying.

If you walk out to the I. P. Pavlová tram stop in the Vinohrady district of Prague on any Saturday morning in summer, you'll find a local flea market—two or three dozen tables featuring a handful of genuine crafts in a sea of tourist crap. I was there with my wife and daughter in July of 2014, when, among the pocket watches and antique postcards and knockoff German pens, the First Republic coins and Russian cigarette lighters, my wife, who's Jewish, came upon a yellow Jewish star. It was in a protective cellophane wrapper like a prized baseball card.

You can't reclaim someone else's past, no matter how fearless your imagination—not really. You can understand perfectly well that there was a particular day, seventy-five years ago, when this piece of cloth in the cellophane wrapper was issued by some representative of the German Reich to someone whose country had been overwhelmed by a tide. That this was absolutely, unquestionably true. You can understand that this man or woman, being Jewish, found themselves doubly marked—the reviled among the conquered. You can imagine the shame, the humiliation, the fear, picture yourself returning home, sewing it on the officially prescribed place on the sleeve thinking, "This is absurd, unbelievable," but it's not you holding the needle while listening to the sounds of the street outside your window, it's not you standing by the window when your wife pricks herself with the needle and starts to cry and can't stop. It's just fucking not.

The past is all around us, but the moment holds itself apart. We can't get there. I don't know that we'd want to, necessarily.

My mother and father were thirteen and fifteen, respectively, when the German army occupied Czechoslovakia. My father was not yet sixteen when he watched that motorcade come through Brno, the Führer, visible only as a visored cap, standing up in his limousine. He was seventeen when he joined the resistance without telling his father, who himself had joined without telling his family. He was twenty-one when, as a cub reporter for *Lidové Noviny*, he was forced to report on the executions that had begun to ramp up in the city. I'll never know what it did to him, where inside of him those hours were buried, whether the trial tempered his soul, or imperceptibly bent it.

In the summer of 1977, I was crossing that same crowded square with my mother when a young man walking toward me clipped my shoulder so hard I nearly fell. He kept walking—no word of apology, no acknowledgment at all. I didn't appreciate it. This wasn't an accidental brush-by in a crowd—this was a sucker punch as a kind of joke.

When I started after him, intending to get an apology, in whatever language, my mother panicked, begged me to let it pass, to forget it, to walk on. Just look at his clothes, she said, clutching my arm. He's German.

I tried to argue—this was 1977, for Christ's's sake, and I was pissed off—but she was genuinely terrified. By now the guy was halfway across the square. I let it go, grudgingly, thinking her ridiculous.

I'm older now. I have more respect for the wells that can open decades after we thought they'd been filled in. My mother had seen the Frauen in their white blouses walking their children to the execution yard at Kounicovy Koleje, lifting them on their shoulders for a better view. She'd seen a man, beaten to the ground, trying to grab the boots of the soldiers stomping him into unconsciousness not five minutes from where we stood. Worse, in some way, her own father, František Kubík, had been a Nazi sympathizer who'd barely escaped death when the war was over. No, I couldn't blame her.

Strangely, the real victim in that episode was the guy in the square. A punk with an attitude, he should have been taken to task, held responsible for his particular misdemeanor, not the high crimes of his country's past. What's the worst that could have happened—a few angry words, at worst a fistfight between nineteen-year-olds? I liked my chances.

Instead he walked on, burdened by association, a murderer by proxy.

The sins of the fathers visit us in curious ways.

IX

NOTHING'S MORE SACRED THAN memory. It's the great, untouchable thing. That stoop I used to sit on with my mother. Her laugh, her smell. My father's big, soft shoulder when he carried me to the car at dawn, lay me down on the back seat, covered me. That night-walk he took me on, his flashlight cutting the gloom like a sword. These things are my essence. My coordinates. They don't have to be good. I'd kill to keep them.

Which is fine, I guess, though I'm troubled by how often loyalty trumps truth when it comes to memory, how the past tends toward uniformity—all this or all that—how revising what I remember, even when it's necessary and just, can feel like the profoundest betrayal. The past clings to me, whispering, "Trust in me beyond thought, believe in me above all things, love me like life itself"—and I have, and continued to, decades after it had been proven false.

And I wonder—is it steadfastness that keeps most of us from questioning our memories, or fear of the pain that that questioning would exact? And if it's fear that keeps us true, how pathetic that devotion is. For some of us, at times, memory is like the Old Testament God: Question me and I will make you suffer; abandon me and I will take your faith.

The problem with being a writer is that well enough won't leave you alone.

I have my memories, drawerfuls of them—they are who I am. Spreading them out on the table, therefore, parsing them, is a kind of self-anatomy. "Uncomfortable" is not the word. I tell myself that this is what writers do, that no one else can hold this scalpel, that the time has come to lay myself down, crack through the rib cage, palp the heart. I tell myself this, but it doesn't help.

It's not fear I have to resist at this moment, but an almost unbearable sense of disloyalty. Even cruelty. I'm betraying her, us, the past. Just leave us alone, she's saying, pleading; leave at least those few memories intact, that handful of golden days when you were still small and the world was still magic and I was everything to you. If you ever loved me, save them. If you respect nothing else, at least respect what was—remember it, and draw a line.

But it's no good, ma. You raised me too well, gave me too much, started undoing your own work a few years too late. It's a different "you" I hear now, the one who, were I to listen, would give me a look of disappointment bordering on disgust. "And you call yourself a writer?" you'd say. "What's the matter, you want people to like you?"

And you'd turn back to your book, dismiss me. It wasn't worth talking about. When it came to writing, there was only one law. It was very simple: Go anywhere. Tell all the truth as you see it.

If I didn't have the guts, I should consider politics.

It's interesting how, once you begin excavating the past, dates change, chronologies adjust. I'd always believed that my mother's descent into madness (though I didn't see it as that for decades) began when I was in my teens; now, the further back I go, the more I remember.

In 1962, when I was three, we learned that my grandmother—my mother's mother—had pancreatic cancer. It had been six months or more since she'd been diagnosed; word had just gotten out.

This was grief multiplied by circumstance, misery squared. My parents had escaped across the Czech border in the winter of 1948 with the aid of a professional smuggler they'd hired to lead them through the forests, to cut through the wire fences—in short, to do whatever needed doing. They knew they were closing the door to home but, like everyone else back then, believed that the new regime could never last, that in a year or two they'd be back. They were wrong. The Communist coup held. A decade passed, another began. News was choked off to a trickle; the occasional letters that came through had been opened and resealed. Fourteen years after my parents' escape, the warrant for their arrest was still active. Returning was unthinkable.

And now my grandmother was dying. There was nothing to do. The sea is the sea, and these drowning men do drown. I may have been a handhold, as children often are. I hope so.

Sometime during those months I sat down with my box of Crayola crayons and drew a creature like a cross between a pig and a crocodile with a long, lizard head full of teeth and a zigzag, poisonous tail. When my mother and father asked, I said it was a *nebezpečny zvíře*—a dangerous animal. I named it *Rakovina*—the Czech word for cancer.

I still remember my mother's joy over that drawing, which now lies buried in one of the boxes crammed with curling photographs and cutout pumpkins and thin *luftpost* envelopes that I've dragged around with me, at considerable cost to my wallet and my back, most of my adult life. Something about that child's conjuring, that literalizing of her fear—something about the fact that even at the age of three I wanted to save her, explain away what was making her sad—opened some kind of channel inside her. I was her boy. I was on her side. She could bear anything.

Years later she'd use that same drawing to gouge her own heart, taking it out of the big, brass-latched steamer trunk she and my father had brought from Australia and holding it up with two fingers like something disgusting—an emblem of my betrayal, a standard to gauge the depth of my fall.

My grandmother, who I never met—who I might have liked, though it's complicated—died that spring. Maybe a month later, my mother came into my room one morning and told me to get dressed. I had to hurry—quickly, quickly. She parted my hair neatly, dressed me in my white shirt and blue shorts, buckled the German sandals that I wasn't yet old enough to despise. I had to hurry. Quickly.

We locked up the apartment and ran down the long, open

corridor that led along the fifteenth floor to the elevator, then down to the lobby and out onto 63rd Road. A hot, smoggy morning like they used to be back then, the air heavy with car exhaust and bakeries and grass, the buildings fading to white in the distance. We turned right toward Queens Boulevard (left meant Waldbaum's), hurrying past the men in their hats and the women in their long, pencil skirts. I was excited, trotting alongside her. Where were we going? I asked at some point.

"To meet your grandmother," my mother said, a kind of disbelieving wonder in her voice. "Hurry—she's waiting for us at Alexander's."

We ran on in the heat. At some point my mother started to slow down, then stopped. She was still holding my hand.

I asked what was the matter.

She didn't say anything. She looked confused. I remember her looking back toward our apartment building, then right toward Alexander's.

"I think we should go home," she said.

And we did.

X

I'VE NEVER LIKED CROSSWORD PUZZLES, probably because I'm bad at them and, like most people, I'm not crazy about things that make me feel stupid. I prefer chess, though I'm not really good at chess either, come to think of it, so maybe it's something else altogether. Maybe it's that crossword puzzles are so preset, so determined. There's only one way to go—five letters, not six, beginning with *d*. How can you breathe in that world?

I was raised in the thickets of human motivation—it's where I feel most at home. It's why the quantifiers, the technocrats, the code writers bent on reducing this wilderness to a logarithm frighten me. In this sense, like many others, I'm my mother's child. She taught me, trained me in paradox, in contradiction, showed me the complicated pleasure of trying to see through the mask. By the time I was nine or ten, she was asking me why such and such a character in a Maugham or Maupassant story had said this or done that, what I thought they really wanted, and why, and whether they knew it themselves. I loved these games, loved her pleasure when I understood something. I was smart—not clever in the British sense of the word, which suggested chattiness, super-fice, a mind like a well-ordered desk—but intuitive in the ways of the human heart and the eternally posing, self-conflicted mind. In short, nobody's fool—unlike Daddy. I believed it. Mommy said so.

Hell, part of me still believes it. In love with many things but ignorant of pretty much everything except growing things, fly-fishing, and, to some extent, literature, I can navigate the canals of self-delusion, say, like nobody's business. The less cer-tain something is, the more I understand it; the less tangible it is, the more readily my fingers grasp it. Just give me a little shove down the byways of regret, and I'm in my element.

Which should make me perfect for the task at hand except that yesterday we started sorting through the cartons of photo-graphs we brought back from my mother's mold-ridden cottage in Moravia ten days ago, separating them off into nine boxes marked "Pre-1930," then progressing on through the decades—40s, 50s, 60s, etc.—and I'm in over my head. There are, quite literally, thousands of them; every fifth or sixth opens a world: my mother as a round-faced infant in 1928, sitting in the grass by the Bečva River in Slovakia; my father with his track team in Brno during the war—all those beautiful young men—in 1941; my parents on board the USS *General Harry Taylor*, en route to Australia—1949. Our house in Ardsley—1967; the Horners on our porch at Twin Lakes, smiling up from their chairs—1970. The decades surge ahead, then vanish: my grandfather as a stern-looking child surrounded by women in Gibson Girl dresses; my daughter, in Leucadia, California, dressed up as a sunflower; my mother, newborn, smothered in lace like an elaborate pastry.

I've always liked untangling things. As a kid, I'd patiently work through the hopeless snarl on my fishing reel rather than cut it loose and refill the reel, because I liked it.

This is different. This nest is a century old and as big as a house—a tangle of lives and stories whose ends have run under the floorboards and into my skin; if I pull a thread, everything tightens, and I feel a pinch, like a stitch pulled before its time.

XI

M IGHT AS WELL BEGIN at the end—because it's not.

On July 6, 2014, my wife and daughter and I traveled from Prague to Brno, Prague's poorer sister to the southeast, to find my mother. On the train, crammed with backpackers bound for Vienna, I talked to a cheerful, elderly couple from Sydney who told me they'd visited the shrine dedicated to the Czech paratroopers who, in 1942, assassinated Reichsprotektor Reinhard Heydrich, the so-called Butcher of Prague—how moved they'd been to see the bullet holes in the chipped wall, the flowers in jars left there by locals who still remembered the day, now three-quarters of a century gone. Nice people, they invited us to visit them in Sydney.

In Brno, we caught a taxi to our hotel, one of those Soviet-era high rises offering the full menu of offenses to proportion and taste: vast, deserted dining rooms perpetually awaiting a party of two hundred; shin-reflecting mirrors on the sides of the "Bowling Bar"; mirrors on walls, on doors, on the elevator ceiling just in case you decided to get it on before you reached your floor or wanted to check the progress of your bald spot. We ate a fine, fatty dinner, then braved the subterranean, –1, level where, by knocking on several locked doors in a white hallway we magically summoned a tall young man dressed like an undertaker who ceremoniously ushered us into the spa featuring multicolored changing lights on the ceiling of the steam room and a whirlpool that drained itself every fifteen minutes.

We laughed. We made jokes about booking a room at the Overlook Hotel, about Jack Nicholson—*Heeeere's Johnny!*—breaking into the bowling bar. I felt better than I had in months. I knew what was coming, or thought I did, but I was ready. At some point, as we sat in the hot tub, a dour, undercooked young man emerged from the sauna, winced over the massage-therapy rocks glued to the floor, then disappeared into the towel room where he proceeded to change, not realizing that the central panel on *this* door, of all the doors in the hotel, wasn't a mirror. Perfect.

In the morning, after a breakfast in the empty dining room featuring a buffet of sausages, breaded meats, cheeses, roasted vegetables, potatoes, etc., large enough to glut a small invading army, we climbed into the rental car and James, the GPS gnome with the reassuring Oxbridge accent ("In one KILO-meetah, tuhn left") led us to my mother who, after a lifetime of exile on three continents, now found herself only a short walk from where she'd been born.

There it was—a pleasant, three-story building on a leafy side street. When we rang the bell, we were welcomed as if we were family. The place was clean, full of light, the nurses large, soft women possessed of that indomitable sense of humor you often find in people who do truly hard things for a living. They seemed warm, genuinely kind. There was a small garden in the courtyard. I could hear birds outside.

Time accelerates. The attention narrows, tunnels. The tag on the door had two names—one I didn't know, and Olga Slouka. My mother.

For a second, maybe two, I didn't understand what I was looking at, and then, as Melville (yet again) once wrote, "reality outran apprehension." She was sitting with her back to us in a bed with a slide-up child's guard like a giant crib. Her legs, protruding from her diaper, were thin as my forearm. Next to her was a stuffed rabbit. She was making a noise I'd never heard before, a kind of prolonged, whining moan. It was the sort of noise you might hear coming from someone deep in sleep, and if you heard it, you'd wake them.

There was nothing to do but go to her, fall to my knees, touch her arm, say her name. It's me, I said, in Czech. Your son. It didn't matter. She was gone. Her eyes looked at me, lost focus, moved on. I could see my wife and daughter standing by the door with their hands over their mouths; the next instant my daughter was by my side, petting her grandmother's arm, talking to her, reminding herself to her.

I didn't cry. I've always been an easy weep: Reading *Old Yeller* to our son when he was five—or was it *Shane?*—I remember struggling against the closing of my windpipe, then pretending I had something in my throat. Yet now, faced with something that could force tears of sympathy from a complete stranger— the tongue moving obscenely as if of its own volition in her half-open mouth, the missing uppers extending her chin into the witch's point of the fairy tales—I didn't cry. It's her, a voice in my head kept saying. *To seš ty*—It's you—I wanted to say to her, so I could believe it. But I didn't. Because it wasn't.

Instead, with the help of one of her nurses who swept into the room like life itself, who sat my mother up, brushed back her hair, then lifted her onto a kind of walker, all the while gabbing away— *You want to take Petřík with you? Well, why not? How're we doing? A little slower?*—we all went down to a cheerful common room with pale yellow curtains where we spent half an hour talking to someone not there.

And it's so strange, as anyone who has gone through it knows, to look into that absence, to wonder if somewhere in that great dark some memories, like bits of dream, still circle. Memories of the two of you together, maybe. Good memories, you hope.

Alas, that would not be my mother's story. No, she'd bring it crashing down, all of it, uncompromised to the bitter end. She'd go hard. No fairy-tale endings here—at least not *those* fairy tales.

Her body, reduced to sixty pounds or so, was going fast, the brain, in its utter helplessness, no longer able to communicate the necessary instructions; she was eating four times a day and starving to death. And the mind? Who's to say, exactly? *Ja se bojím*, she kept saying over and over again in that sun-filled room overlooking the garden. I'm afraid. There's nothing to be afraid of, Mom, I kept repeating, stroking her hand, which she seemed to like. There's nothing to be afraid of.

Ja se bojím, she'd repeat in that whiny, child-robot voice I could barely recognize.

There's nothing to be afraid of, Mom. Look—Petřík is here, we're here.

Ja se bojím.

Everything's fine, Mom.

Ja se bojím.

What is it, Mom? What are you afraid of?

She paused.

Ja nevím—I don't know.

There's nothing to be afraid of, I repeated, idiotically, because I didn't know what else to say, because I needed to convince myself. There's nothing to be afraid of. What are you afraid of?

She paused again, the tongue turning and prodding as if the answer was something she'd find in her mouth.

Tell me what you're afraid of, Mom, I said again, holding her hand.

And she looked at me with those watery eyes, lost, not recognizing me, her only child. But she'd found it.

Zlo, she said, and I thought I saw a flash of her old self, dug in deep at the end of the world. Evil.

Two days later, I went back. I had to. I sat with her for five minutes, talked to her about the stuffed lion we'd brought, which seemed to have made friends with the monkey, which was resting its head on the lion's shoulder.

Then I kissed her on her head, then once more—that thin, familiar hair, that scent that was hers alone in this world— and left.

XII

IN THE MID-1970S WHEN I was sixteen, seventeen, eighteen years old, I'd travel to Czechoslovakia, the country my parents had grown up in, escaped from, and would eventually return to, and during these visits I'd sometimes take the tram to see my great-uncle Pepa and my great-aunt Sonya.

This was still a decade and a half before the unimaginable, pickup-sticks collapse of the Soviet Union, fifteen years before the Velvet Revolution gave back to Czechoslovakia the sovereign right of every nation to foul its nest in its own way. Václav Havel was still a dissident playwright, foreigners had to report to the authorities within forty-eight hours of crossing the border, the stores were more or less empty—except, of course, for those reserved for the elect. You watched what you said, where you said it, who you said it to—if not for your sake, then for the sake of those speaking to you, who in any case would have to fill out a special form reporting that they'd had contact with someone from the West and explaining the reason for it.

Perversely, maybe because I was young, or because the blue

passport in my back pocket protected me from most humiliations and risks, I have wonderful memories of that time. It was undeniably exciting, full of intrigue, rich in subtext, innuendo, double-speak. I felt like a secret agent. As a kid from New York, one who spoke Czech, no less, I was a curiosity, which was almost like being popular—a new experience for me. I didn't mind.

I liked prerevolution Czechoslovakia. I liked the otherness of it, the smell of plaster and coal smoke, the courtyards with their plots of lettuces and kohlrabi, the rabbit hutches stacked under the eave. I loved the electrical smell of the trams, the lonely Moravian forests into which I'd disappear with a book, a hammock and a couple of rohlíky and cheese. I liked figuring things out, jumping on lines whenever they formed on the sidewalk because there was bound to be something desirable—oranges from Croatia, say, or batteries from Poland, or a new translation of *The Trial*—at the end of them. I fell in love—with a girl, yes, but with a country as well—and three or four times a summer I'd spend an afternoon at my great-aunt and -uncle's, where my aunt would stuff me like a Christmas pig.

Of course they're gone now—they were old even then. And yet, though that house has belonged to someone else for half a lifetime, I still see them there as vividly as if it were 1975 and I'd just stepped outside to use the outhouse. It's been only a minute or two, and I push open the back door and walk through the dark living room into the tiny kitchen and there they are—my aunt standing with her back to me by the stove, mixing something with her knobbed, arthritic hands, my uncle with his grizzled block of a head sitting at the table, the two of them grown into one another so completely that to think of them at all was to think of one person, not two.

Those were good days. For some reason it always seemed to be raining when I visited them—I remember cold drops on the back of my neck and the smell of wet leaves on the way to the outhouse—and when we sat in the kitchen and talked, the overgrown windows, steamed up from the cooking, would turn into runny Japanese prints—stems and leaves, green bleeding into gray. It was as if our roles had been predetermined for ages. They'd always have already eaten. My aunt, to whom the words "I swear I can't eat another bite" were like spurs to a racehorse, would stand by the stove and cook, only occasionally adding some detail to something being said. I'd gorge myself and listen. My uncle would sit across from me, his big shoulders hunched up over the tiny kitchen table, and talk.

I want to believe that each of us has someone who will take us in—always, no matter what. In my life, along with one or two others, I had Uncle Pepa and Aunt Sonya.

I'd like to be them someday, for somebody else.

Theirs was a good story, and like all good stories, it didn't sit easy. Who knows, now, how much of it I heard from them, how much from others? I'm not sure it matters. If some of the names and dates are off, the whole remains true, anchored by things I heard and touched.

It began with my uncle's medals from the First World War,

which he kept in a tin box in a drawer in the living room bureau. They were an impressive bunch, and there were a lot of them, acknowledging, as I recall, my uncle's bravery, his selflessness, his willingness to pay the ultimate price for the sake of whoever it was, exactly, that had asked for it. Now this one, he'd say, shaking it loose from the tangled mess with his thick fingers, is one of the highest commendations the Russian Army conferred on its soldiers—and he'd toss it aside like an old spoon and reach for another. This one, he'd chuckle, is for courage under fire. When we came to the ones written in Cyrillic, my aunt would come over and translate.

When I asked him if he'd mind telling me about his experiences in the war, he said he didn't mind at all, though he was worried that, being young and impressionable and from America, I'd take it all too much to heart. He was no hero, he assured me modestly, but a man like any other.

I told him I understood, accepted another slice of my aunt's walnut cream cake, and he began.

I don't remember many of the details—how my uncle, at sixteen, was drafted into the Austro-Hungarian Army, where exactly on the Russian front he was sent, which general he fought under. (Given that the Czechs were less than thrilled to be fighting for the Germans *against* their fellow Slavs confuses the picture still more.) Enough that he was sixteen, a strong, likable kid fond of girls and gymnastics—the parallel bars were his specialty—and that he was going to war.

It all went ridiculously quickly. Issued boots, a mess kit and a rifle—a single-shot, lever-action affair—he suddenly found himself, after a few days of calisthenics and a long train ride, standing with his comrades on the edge of an enormous untilled field broken by small clumps of trees and told to charge—the enemy was just ahead, they were told, massed behind the trees—which he did.

Everything went perfectly, he said, until the men running next to him began to fall, at which point he woke up. People were dying all around him. The noise was terrible. He wanted no part of this, my uncle said, and so, still clutching his gun, he flung himself theatrically into a thicket and pretended to be dead. He had no idea how long he lay there—a long time. At some point he had to sneeze, he remembered, but smothered it; at another, his left leg just behind the knee began to itch so vindictively that he'd have gladly ripped his skin off with his own nails to get at it. Eventually—he was lying partly on his side, face down—he managed to twitch just enough, spacing out the slight, spastic movements by agonizing minutes, to bring one knee behind the other, and scratch. When everything was quiet, he carefully looked around and, finding the field empty except for the dead, started walking south. He was almost 1,200 kilometers from Brno. He'd had enough of soldiering.

He would have made it, too, he said, if it hadn't been for the goddamn rifle. It was a beauty, and walking down a deserted country road the next morning, he began thinking what a shame it was that he'd never shot it. Not once. In fact, he wasn't entirely sure he knew *how* to shoot it—they must have assumed everyone knew, and anybody who didn't had been too ashamed to admit it—but he figured it out, took aim at a sign thirty or forty meters away, and fired.

The gun went off with a satisfying roar, which would have been fine except for the force of Russian soldiers resting in a wrinkle in the landscape a hundred meters away who, admiring the sound, stood up as if out of the earth and promptly took my sixteen-year-old great-uncle prisoner for the crime of stupidity. The first, last and only shot he fired in the Great War, he said, was at a road sign. He missed.

And so the war hero was taken prisoner, though whatever notions I might have in my head about Russian prison camps, I should forget them—this was not that. A two-room village prison, a good bed, blankets, decent food. The commanding officer, a gruff, modestly literate man in his early forties capable of doing his duty while appreciating the absurdity of keeping a sixteen-year-old prisoner—let's call him Commander Žižkov—took a liking to him: The boy had a good attitude, a strong back. . . . If he'd had a son, he wouldn't have minded if he was like him.

A few months passed. My uncle was picking up some Russian, which is not all that far from Czech; the two would talk. About the war, about the October Revolution, about food. Was he a good student back home in Brno? Hardly, my uncle said. What he really loved was gymnastics.

Really? Žižkov said. What sort of gymnastics?

My uncle didn't have the words, but he pantomimed the disciplines well enough to be understood: the parallel bars, tumbling—

most of all he said, patting his heart then laying his head on his hands like a lovesick girl, he loved the rings, and standing in his cell, he assumed an expression of great effort and stretched his arms straight out from his body like Christ. Žižkov was impressed. The iron cross? You can do this? Christ poked his own chest three times with his finger. Absolutely.

The next afternoon Žižkov came by and unlocked my uncle's cell. He was to come with him. This war might go on a while, he explained, and meanwhile his daughter, fifteen years old, was crazy for gymnastics. For the foreseeable future, therefore, he had arranged (with whom, he didn't say) for my great-uncle to be released three times a week after school hours for gymnastics lessons until such time as his daughter's interests shifted to something else—was that understood?

And so, three times a week through the coming winter and the following spring, my now-seventeen-year-old Great-Uncle Pepa walked through the snow to the school at the end of the village where he gave the commander's daughter, who turned out to be a fine tumbler, gymnastics lessons, then walked back and let himself into his cell. Two months after armistice was declared, they were married. A month after that, my Great-Aunt Sonya kissed her family goodbye—by now her father may have had some regrets about the gymnastics lessons—and left with him on the train to Warsaw, from there to Vienna, and from Vienna to Brno, which at that time might as well have been one of Jupiter's sixty-seven moons. She planned to see them again, talked of it for years, but as far as I know, never did.

How my Great-Uncle Pepa came by the Red Army medals,

I haven't a clue. Maybe they were a wedding gift of some sort: *Here, these may be useful someday.* It makes no sense, except that it happened.

And the years grew into decades, filled with the sedimentary business of living—trips to the marketplace or to visit my uncle's relatives, Sunday mornings in bed or in the garden, evenings in the kitchen, making plans—punctuated now and then by bigger events both happy and not. A son was born to them. Across town, a half-hour's tram ride away, my great-uncle's sister (my grandmother, Luba) and her husband, František, had a daughter. There were June picnics on the grassy slopes of the Přehrada, Brno's great, miles-long reservoir, summer vacations to the Moravian forests or the Tatra Mountains in Slovakia. In 1932, my great-aunt Kateřina, who'd always been willful, sat down on a bench opposite the apartment of the married man with whom she'd been having an affair and drank a bottle of lye to teach him a lesson, burning out her throat and a good part of her esophagus. A trained nurse getting off the tram from work, seeing a woman thrashing on the sidewalk trying to strangle herself with her own hands, saved her—how I don't know—thereby unknowingly rescuing her husband's lover, someone she'd convinced herself she'd imagined. Kateřina, who loved cats as much as she despised my maternal grandfather—who banned her from his house for life—would live to scare little children with her throaty croak another thirty years.

And so it went. By all accounts Pepa and Sonya's marriage was a good one—better than good—though not unmarked by the usual strains and misunderstandings. The great unsolvable thing, apparently, was Sonya's homesickness, which would come over her with a flu-like violence—often brought on by nothing more than a scent—linger, then leave. There was nothing her husband could do at these times but comfort her, and, in fact, she never asked him for anything more, the two of them having recognized these attacks of nostalgia as something to be lived with, like occasional heart palpitations, or headaches. Sonya would cry; sometimes, alone in the house, or out in the garden, she'd whisper to herself in Russian, a language whose accents still softened her imperfect Czech fifty years later—and then she'd stop.

Who can really tell what life was like for them—what measure of happiness was theirs, what needs in each other they met or failed, what compromises they made with whatever dreams they might have had. When I think of them now, I see them as figures in a child's diorama, the city of Brno laid out with cardboard buildings and benches and miniature trolleys, except that this diorama—unlike the exhibits at the Art Institute of Chicago, where I'd spend hours peering into the fist-sized rooms, trying to read the titles of the books next to the woman knitting behind the fingernail-sized leaded window—this diorama is complete down to the silver-powder smear of a moth crushed against the curtains and, more important, set to time. All history is here, and when the precise moment comes, the machinery whirs, the gears mesh, and a character sitting frozen in his chair takes a sip from his cup.

It's 1925, a February thaw, the powdered-sugar snow pulling back against the walls and fences. My grandmother, Luba, is lying in bed, trying to shush her day-old daughter, whom they've named

Olga, who looks like something boiled. To my grandmother, who was told she couldn't bear children and who will never have another, she's a miracle. You'll be everything I'm not, she whispers. And she begins to hum, as if on cue, a tune she hasn't thought of in years. My grandfather knocks, then enters. Isn't she beautiful? my grandmother says. Neatly dressed in a white shirt and vest, clean-shaven, his bottle-brush hair still black, my thirty-one-year-old grandfather stands by the bed, one hand in his pocket, looking down at his daughter. I think she's sleeping, my grandmother says, and he nods, almost imperceptibly, agreeing with something else, then reaches out and touches the three middle fingers of his left hand to the baby's head as if taking her temperature.

One by one the rooms fire like carousels, characters stir and rise and walk. Pepa's father, the patriarch with the white handlebar mustache, furious over the obstinacy of one of his cherry trees, climbs off the ladder at the age of ninety-four and, seating himself on the offending branch, calmly saws himself off. A woman is rolling on the sidewalk, clutching her throat. My mother, a seven-year-old little girl with a quick smile and a tender heart, sees a dog's hindquarters cut off by a train in Slovakia. Meanwhile, over here, overlooked by everyone, the janitor of 46 Zahradníková Street and his wife have had a son of their own, and my father begins the twenty-one-year dance that will bring him into my mother's life, and mine.

XIII

AND SO MY AUNT AND UNCLE, sitting in that kitchen with the rain heavy on the windows, telling their tales. I can see my uncle's huge, knobbed hands, feel the dusty softness of my aunt's cheek against my lips. I can smell the *koprová*—cream sauce with dill, my favorite— warming on the stove. When I think of that kitchen, I see the display at the Museum of Natural History showing chipmunks sleeping in a stomach-shaped cell two feet under the snow-covered ground, and I realize that those hours—the sound of their voices, our bodies brushing by each other in that cramped space, even the smell of the dill sauce—were so precious because they were nested inside a barely held-off poverty, warmed by the crumbling plaster in the corner by the stove, by my uncle's cracked heels showing above his thinned-out slippers, by the metal edge of the kitchen table pulling away from the cheap linoleum top.

Memories sit well as long as they're of a piece, organic, rising like an inverted genealogy, trunk to branch to leaf. It's only when a harder story intrudes—when somebody comes along and pounds a nail into your narrative, so to speak—that the work of reconciling begins. It's not easy. You have to grow around the offending bit, absorb it into your story.

Sometimes it's easier to deny the part that doesn't fit. Always, actually. Which is called lying to yourself (and others) for the sake of consistency.

For most of my life, whenever I thought of my Uncle Pepa and my Aunt Sonya—when I recalled the way they'd move around each other in that small kitchen, reaching out to touch a shoulder or a hip as unconsciously as a blind person navigates a familiar room; or the way their minds, like children racing down a forest path, would diverge and come together, one moving ahead, then the other taking over; or even the way an occasional look, even at their age, suggested an intimacy I could barely understand—I saw them as very nearly the perfect couple. There, right in front of my eyes—unsanctimonious, unirritating—was the thing that everyone wanted: a genuine, passionate, enduring marriage, grounded in mutual respect and, might as well say it, love.

This is what I thought. I still do.

And yet.

The wider frame. Much wider: Berchtesgaden, Bad Godesberg, Berlin. All those *B*'s. Neville Chamberlain steps from his limousine. President Beneš of Czechoslovakia, shouted down by Hitler, rushes from the room, visibly trembling, shaken by this breach of all civility, all decency, all previous protocol.

The year is 1938. Arguments are made. Tea is sipped. Various men stab their fingers at the polished table. *"Sie müssen . . . Wir werden."* In Bad Godesberg, Chamberlain smoothes his hair with his right hand and says "I take your point, Herr Ribbentrop. And yet, if I may . . . we feel that . . . in the matter of . . . Can I take that as your final position?" And it comes to pass. On March 15, 1939, in an official radio message in some ways as unbelievable to those listening to it as the formal announcement of their own deaths, Czechoslovakia ceases to exist. The message is delivered in the declarative, staccato tones of an authority accustomed to ruling by decree, to establishing fact by fiat: Bohemia and Moravia are henceforth the Protektorat Böhmen und Mähren, under the control of the Reichsprotektor; Slovakia is an "independent" state under the German-backed Catholic clergyman Jozef Tizo. There's no ambiguity: adjust or die.

Three days later, on March 18, my father, not yet sixteen years old, stands by the window waiting for Hitler's motorcade to pass through Brno. Peeking between the heavy blue curtains is like looking into an aquarium. A deep, unnatural silence fills the city; all public transportation has been stopped, all automobile traffic forbidden. People linger in the hallways of their apartment buildings, saying little. Military loudspeakers echo outside, announcing that all windows onto the street are to remain closed until 2 p.m. By nine-thirty, the city of Brno is deserted.

The motorcade passes quickly, headed north—fifteen or twenty black limousines surrounded by twice as many motorcycles, tight as a swarm. Hitler's personal limousine, an open car, perhaps fifth in line, is slightly apart from the others. Hitler himself, when my father sees him, is just sitting down, his features from that second-floor window—except for a quick glimpse of jaw and mustache—almost completely obscured by the visor of his military cap.

And just like that, the moment's gone, leaving behind a new order, a new reality. It will remain in place for six years. Some will be permitted to endure it. Many will not. My aunt and uncle will be among the lucky ones; they'll work their garden, keep low, survive. And through it all, since our private worlds don't shut down in the face of public events, my aunt will continue to quietly miss her country, her language, whispering to herself in her mother tongue even as the news of Russian victories begins to filter through, even as the unbreakable granite block of the Reich—pounded by the Allies in the West, worn down by an unanswerable river of bodies in the East—begins to crack: first nothing, then a hairline split like a mineral seam, then a sudden tree, leaping into bloom. It will give.

I understand my aunt in those years. I do. I understand the voluptuousness of nostalgia, that need to pull out the past like a letter that still carries the scent—or so you imagine—of someone you loved. I understand that infidelity to the present, not only because my mother, inheriting the gene, raised the art of regret to a masochistic pitch I've never seen equaled, but because I tend that way myself. I don't take kindly to loss.

When I was fourteen, my mother and father told me that we'd given up our cabin on Lost Lake, a place I carried inside me like blood. I didn't say anything. I didn't have a vote. But I didn't accept it, either. For weeks, instead of reconciling myself, building new loves, I'd spend the afternoon hours in a plastic fold-ing chair in our stifling yard in Bethlehem, Pennsylvania, remem-bering, recreating—I want to say reconstituting, as though I were adding water to things that would fatten and wave in the thick summer air—every inch of that lost shoreline, every fallen tree, every stone, smelling the sweet rotting smell of the coves, watch-ing the water shadows crawling up the trunks of the oaks, hearing the thin scrape of a painted turtle pulling itself up on a log until, now and then, for a second only, by some miracle of memory as painful as it was exhilarating, I was there. No, I can understand my Aunt Sonya very well indeed.

It's what happened next that I have a little trouble with.

The war ended, quietly, unambiguously, like the fine breath of rot raised by a thaw, exactly on April 26, 1945. It wasn't much, my father said: no Soviet tanks bucking across the soaking fields, just one man on horseback, a Cossack, at dawn, watching his reflec-tion passing in the dark windows, riding slowly up Zejrová Street to the foot of the vineyards, then slowly back.

After him came others, two, three at a time. This was the lib-eration: no regiments, no heavy artillery. German snipers still held the hills outside Brno. At night they would aim at the Soviet sol-diers silhouetted against the fires of boards and bench slats blazing in the road until some of the men, my father's father among them, couldn't stand it anymore and went out and said for the love of god stay to the side, why die for no reason? And apparently—so the story goes—one of them looked up from where he squatted by the flames, then out into the vague darkness, then back to the fire. *Da nicego. Nas mnogo,* he said. It's nothing—there are many of us. My grandfather had already crossed the street when the man spoke again, not looking up from the fire. "Hide your women, old man. We're not the last."

The *havět'*, the vermin (General Malinowski's troops), came later. *Špína*, my father called them, dirt, the after-scum of the general army: illiterate, ragged, undisciplined, many of them two and three years on the front. They moved through from the southeast, a bestial tide, monstrously unpredictable, unafraid to die. Some, like stunned children, were capable of small, absurd gestures of generosity. Some gobbled toothpaste, squeezing it on their bread like pâté. My grandfather, hearing the sound of breaking glass and the crash of piano keys, came downstairs to find one, pants pulled down around his ankles, crapping in the baby grand. When he was done, he left. Some raped a ten-year-old girl. She died. My nineteen-year-old mother, buried in the coal pile in the cellar by her father, survived.

Aunt Sonya didn't see any of this because she was gone. Not dead, not kidnapped—gone. Swept up. Overcome.

I don't know how it happened—where the soldiers met her, what she said, whether she was working in the garden or waiting for a tram. I'll never know what things, exactly, in what proportion, drove her, how much of it was seeing her years of nostalgia suddenly made flesh, how much of it was the sound of those tongue-softened consonant phonemes, how much some deep dissatisfaction with my uncle and how much the straight-shot erotic rush (sorry, aunt) of being desired by hard men possessed of a certain ruthless charm. I'll never know. What I *do* know is that at that time and place, at the end of that particular war, my Aunt

Sonya's answer to the question *Would you forsake your house and home?* was, "Yes, I would. I will. I have."

This I also know: that when my Great-Uncle Pepa returned home that rainy afternoon in the spring of 1945 to find his wife missing, a neighbor braver than most told him everything: that they'd been Russian soldiers, that he didn't know the division or regiment they belonged to, that they'd headed north, that Sonya hadn't appeared unwilling. That she hadn't reacted when he and his wife had shouted out to her. And my uncle nodded, packed a bag, and, unarmed, left to find his wife.

I heard it took him nine days. I have no reason to doubt it. The miracle is that he found her at all in the chaos of the liberation. It couldn't have been easy. He spoke some Russian, and that helped, but it must have been hard inquiring after his wife like a missing bicycle that had decided to roll off on its own, explaining to commanders who, after all, had bigger things on their minds, like a war just passed, that no, his wife hadn't been kidnapped, that no, he had no idea, really, why she'd left though she'd missed her home, that no, he'd never been unkind to her, or inattentive (ignoring the smiles, the occasional smirks), that yes, in spite of everything, no matter what she'd done, if she wanted to return, he'd have her back. It must have been hard following lead after lead, sleeping in haylofts like a tramp, walking down roads still alive with troop movements (an urban man, he had no car), accepting rides once or twice in military vehicles and once on the back of a sympathetic (or pitying) soldier's horse. It couldn't have been easy—none of it. I don't believe he cared.

In my mind I see a small encampment by a rain-swollen river

but really, I have no clue where it was, or what time of day, whether a fine misty spring rain was falling or whether he found her in someone's camp bed or just stirring the soup—all I know is that he found her and told her it was time to come home if she wanted to come home, and that she said she did and that the soldiers didn't shoot either of them but let her go and she came away with him as easily as she'd left him. And they started off on the long walk home to Brno.

Every marriage is forged differently; some crack at a touch, others endure beyond belief, still others are tempered by events and time. My guess is that my great-aunt's and -uncle's marriage was made on that walk back home, that lying next to each other in the hay-smelling dark somewhere along the way, they were able to dig into that soil of omissions and misunderstandings and regrets out of which this thing had grown, and make things right.

How else can I reconcile my aunt's adventure with the marriage that followed it—how else incorporate that nail into the narrative?—except to see those days as not only something they survived, but as the very thing that allowed them to endure— that made them who they were? No, of this I'm sure: Over those two weeks some imbalance had been violently corrected and, like a broken bone set true, they'd healed stronger. Not because my uncle turned his face like Christ and forgave her—because that kind of self-abnegation, or is it condescension? would only engender pity, or disgust—but because he recognized in the events that had overtaken them a purging and forgivable necessity, the kind of storm that could clear the air for a lifetime or more.

XIV

I KNEW THEM. I knew them in that way of knowing that goes so far back you can hear the keel scrape off the shore of memory into that strange dark before you.

I remember almost everything about my father, though he's been gone a while now, at least in the way we measure going. I remember his face, his eyes, his thin straight hair, his laborer's hands with the yellowed, clamshell fingernails putting the lie to decades of professing. I remember his insecurities and his enthusiasms and his peasant endurance which looks, from where I am now, very much like strength. I remember his voice, which two years after his death—the anniversary is tomorrow—still cuts my heart.

But my father's easy. Not because I knew him better, or because he was easier to know. Because he loved me, particularly in the later years. Because he loved those I loved. Because he and I came to accept ourselves in a way that let us both live our lives. Doesn't get much simpler than that.

Nothing about my mother was easy. Nothing. Sitting at the window of our cabin at Lost Lake (I returned, years later, because

I don't take kindly to loss) just a five-minute walk from where she and I spent the summers of my childhood nearly half a century ago, I can see the pasture wall someone built with a mule and a stone boat generations before I was born angling down between the oaks, then disappearing into water that wasn't there then. And I know that some things change while others stay the same as the world changes around them, but that's all I know.

As a kid, I'd follow the wall down into the lake. On hot summer days, with the cicadas sawing in the heat, I'd balance over the rocks, then out into the water soupy with tiny moths and gnats and purple loosestrife blossoms, knee- then thigh- then waist-deep, eventually dog-paddling, feeling around with my toes for the top of the wall below me. Now and then, thirty or forty or fifty yards out, I'd bump into that unexpected higher boulder, and stand, imagining someone on the shore seeing me rise up from the lake as if lifted on the back of some invisible thing.

When I try, I can hear my mother's voice. Her face, for some reason, is harder, maybe because photographs have filled in for memory. Just now, as I wrote the previous paragraph, a lullaby she used to sing returned to me, every word, as if it had been resting somewhere. And for just those few seconds, mixed with the tidal sound of the September wind in the oaks, I heard her singing and, inevitably, like falling down a flight of stairs, I remembered loving her as she was then, forcing me to take off my glasses and rub my eyes to clear the words on the page.

What was it all about then, all that love and rage? What did it add up to, and what did it cost? Who betrayed whom? And what happens to those left standing on the field of days—what do they do?

They say you have to come to terms with the past. An odd expression—it has such a martial feeling to it. You imagine banners in the wind, unfurled scrolls, peace in exchange for territory. Which sounds about right.

There's a place in Greece, a region of stone and olive groves and salt pools, that kept itself in equilibrium for centuries, they say, by adhering to the logic of the blood feud. At regular intervals, one family would declare war on another and a long, slow war of attrition would begin until, years or decades later, its rock fields mounded with the dead, one side would petition for mercy. So far, so good—the madness of our species is nothing new.

Attached to this recognizable horror, though, was a footnote: If an individual killed someone from another family, apart from any larger feud, and it was proved that this had been done by accident, or in a state of drunkenness, the killer could make amends by dedicating himself to his victim's family, becoming their benefactor and protector. And often a lifelong regard, even love, would grow between the family of the murdered son or husband or father and the murderer who'd adopted them, something both extraordinarily beautiful and terribly sad.

But I wonder about it. Did you remember the son you'd lost—and if you did, how could you bear it? Was your love for his murderer an act of homage—or did you, in effect, murder him a second time by accepting the man who'd killed him into your heart? Most amazingly, how could the murderer not come to hate his victim's family for what he'd done to them? Forgiving those who trespass against us is a piece of cake; forgiving those we've trespassed against, well, that's another story.

"Look out for those who do you wrong," my mother would tell me, "because they'll hate you for it; every time they look at you, you'll remind them of the kind of person they are." The reverse was also true: "Allow someone to do you a kindness, and they'll love you for it, because you allow them to think well of themselves."

She wasn't wrong. She just wasn't entirely right. In my mother's world, hate, like love, deepened like a coastal shelf; she didn't allow for the islands lying just beneath the surface.

XV

So my aunt and uncle made their way home, walked into their house, began the rest of their lives. It would take a while for the bubble to return to plumb—my aunt's transgression had been a big one—but from the beginning there were two things in her favor: She'd run away with Russian soldiers, who, despite the depredations of Malinowski's troops, were still seen as liberators (had she run away with German soldiers, there would have been no coming back), and she herself was Russian, which not only made her "other," but to some extent excused her actions; most of her neighbors could credit the madness that the memory of home could induce.

Still, she'd be made to suffer for a while—the salacious parts had to be pecked at and clucked over. How utterly had she abandoned herself? they worried. Would there be a child? Had she slept with one, or all; in sequence or at once? And though some—women in particular—would always assume the worst, and spend years furiously embroidering the image, talking about it in tones of disgust laced with envy, my mother, who loved Sonya, was never among them. Sonya, she maintained, was a good and decent woman, humanized by her transgression, not diminished by it, surrounded by hypocrites and clods deaf to their own hearts or lacking them entirely—she'd defend her to the end of her life. Who among us could say when the past would come knocking, or what shape it would take? Who could predict the extent to which our compromises had prepared us for its coming? No, given the right combination of things, anyone could fall.

I agreed with her then, as I agree with her now. And if it's impossible for me not to see an element of self-justification in her embrace of my aunt, that doesn't lessen the value of her loyalty. Charity is rarely disinterested, and rarely ennobled when it is; forgiving others is a way of forgiving ourselves—because it's easier that way. No, I'm grateful for any measure of self-forgiveness my mother was able to find. She deserved it.

The war was over. It would be nice to believe that in the spring of 1945, for a while at least, life returned to its bed. It wasn't so. Before the liberation was even over, the reprisals had begun; you don't oppress a people for six years—or, in the case of Czech sympathizers, cheer on the oppressors—without paying for it when the tables turn. Some of the beatings, evictions, seizures of property, were richly justified. Others—because nothing about being a victim automatically confers virtue, and because cruelty is easily masked as moral outrage—were not.

I believe that my grandfather's hanging, had it come to pass, might have ranked among the justified, but it did not come to pass for the simple reason that my uncle Pepa, on hearing from his frantic sister that my collaborationist grandpa had been dragged from the house, beaten, then thrown in jail to await his fate—which wouldn't take its time in coming—dressed himself in his soldier's uniform, tucked his box of Russian Army medals under his arm and went to save the bastard who had married his sister. And managed it, somehow, though forgiveness was not in the air that June, and he himself would probably have been just fine with letting things take their course. As would I.

And suddenly he's here, peering between the lines, forcing them apart. I've tried to hold him off, partly out of cowardice, partly because releasing him means exposing so much, so quickly—entire lives, including my own. But it might as well be now.

The diorama begins to buckle, then burn.

XVI

To get to him, I have to go through her, which is ironic and just. I have to work backwards, trace the burn patterns to the arsonist's match.

When I was a kid growing up in Rego Park, or during the long summers at Lost Lake, my mother and I weren't just close. We were in league with each other, soulmates, a church of two. We saw the world from the same angle, laughed at the same things. Beauty and pain entered us simultaneously, easily—the pull of the bow across a violin string, the taste of blackberries hot from the sun, the scene in *The Jungle Book* in which Mowgli, crying now as men do, must leave the jungle.

Unlike my father, the rationalist, the clod, who never closed his eyes while listening to a song, never felt without thinking first, never loved. Not really. Who couldn't even cry when his own father died but received the news, went to bed, fell asleep, while she herself—can you believe it?—spent all night tossing in a sea of grief. A good man in many ways—my mother didn't mean to say he wasn't, he was my father after all, and he had his strengths, she wouldn't hear a word said against him—just a little weak. It wasn't his fault. Different men simply had different strengths. Once, back in Australia, someone had referred to him as a *splasklá bublina*—literally a "popped bubble," though "flaccid balloon" is better—which was cruel, but, well, not entirely off the mark, either.

Christ, how we laughed at him, the intellectual in his horn-rim glasses, always a beat behind, missing the joke, mishearing the lyric, giving away the secret; my father, who had no sense of style, no dash; who could be counted on to get wrong what any truly confident man would get right by instinct.

Some men just had it, my mother said. Others didn't. Yul Brynner, with that steely gaze, that voice, that long smooth walk, had it. Steve McQueen, all catlike grace and cool, self-deprecating confidence, had it. It was something instinctive, innate, danger-ous and unmistakably attractive: an inner barrier, a ruthlessness, a point past which no one could push. This barrier was never revealed, never alluded to—there was no bluster involved, no posing—others simply sensed it in you.

My mother had it, this inner strength, this frontier beyond which no negotiation was possible—a fact made clear in the story of the wartime peach.

It might have been 1942, or '43, a time of terrible food short-ages in the cities, and my mother had somehow come into posses-sion of a peach—a rarity, a treasure. In the story, my mother and father are walking along a slow river, arguing, when something my twenty-year-old father says bumps into "it"—the wall beyond which no negotiation is possible. Speaking not in anger but with the steely determination, if not the voice, of Yul Brynner in *The Magnificent Seven*, my mother tells my father that if he says this thing one more time, she'll throw the peach into the river. It's not a threat, it's a promise. My father, not realizing of course where he's found himself, unaware of this Maginot Line in her character (after all, how could he be expected to recognize it?), aware only of the self-defeating idiocy of flinging away something so precious, calls her bluff. And my mother throws the peach across the water and into the trees, and my father, at that moment, glimpses in this girl a strength he's never known, can't understand, and sure as hell ain't got.

I grew up with that story. It was told to me more than once, and told well; I even seem to remember my father being there for the telling. But I wonder now if a peach, even in times of food shortages and food requisitions by the Gestapo, would be quite that valuable in a town of backyard gardens, and how, if it was that valuable, my mother would have come by it—did my father give it to her?—and how, finally, the two of them would have been out walking almost two years before they met.

But no worries—the story was what it was, and I never thought to question it, probably because I didn't want to. You see, I was one of those—like Yul Brynner or Steve McQueen—who would throw the peach. It was obvious, my mother said. I had the strength. She could see it in me. Which would have been fine, I suppose—kids grow into the imaginings of their parents all the time—except that none of this was about me. Not really. At least, not yet.

The story of the peach—and how crude, how obvious, it seems to me now—fed like a tributary into the bedroom, that dark, inland sea. Manliness implied a certain ruthlessness of soul; it was about having a limit. If Steve McQueen said he'd shoot you if you said something again, your choice was simple. When my parents fought, my mother would often lock herself in the bedroom and sometimes my father, bellowing, goaded like a bull into a kind of helpless fury, would pound on the door with his fists, threatening to break it down.

He never did—and my mother despised him for it. He was rational—he'd be the one who'd have to fix it. He was weak. By the time I was fourteen I understood that my father didn't understand women, that there were some men, poor souls, who never quite admitted to themselves who they were; really, she'd admire him more if he had the strength to face up to his nature. And, deserter that I was—but why didn't he talk to me, fight for me?— I'd agree with her.

The man who breaks down the door; I can recognize the misogynistic cliché, the circa 1950 cinematic swoon—Eva Marie Saint's fists pounding on Marlon Brando's chest in mock resistance, "Oh, you big brute!"—even leave the PC police entirely behind and happily acknowledge that human beings draw their sexual current from all kinds of sources, many of them powerful in direct proportion to their dangerousness, and still be sickened by how quickly, in this case, the scene goes bad. If sexuality is like the human heart, constantly beating in systolic/diastolic rhythm, drawing from and coloring our world, now and then something goes very wrong: the heart beats poison. It won't stop until it stops.

I don't want to trace this tributary, which deepens, unnaturally, the closer you get to its source, but I will. Not because I want to, but because there's no one else, and justice requires it. The poet would remember, Czeslaw Milosz once wrote. It didn't matter how many you killed, another would be born to expose your crimes.

I'm no poet. Still.

It's taken me forty years to understand what I was being told—what it was she was trying to tell me—*if* she was trying. She touched on it four, maybe five, times in my life. She was never clear. Stunningly, I never thought to ask, to push her. I don't know why. It may be unforgivable, and now it's too late, though as I write this I wonder if, even today, I'd have the courage to force her through that door, or whether I'd hesitate, worried I'd be doing more harm than good. Is there a point beyond which the well-examined life turns into cruelty?

There was "that day," she'd say. That day her mother came unexpectedly into her room. When she was nineteen. Her father was in the room with her. All hell broke loose—there was a terrible scene.

That's it—that's all I have. But I have the aftershock, the echo. You don't need to see the bomb to understand the carnage in the marketplace. My grandmother took charge. My mother had been dating a boy—someone she barely knew. Within three weeks they were married, a marriage made easy by the fact that my mother—

young, beautiful, solidly middle-class—was marrying the son of
a former janitor. The man was my father.

It gets worse. Within a month of the wedding, my grandmother arranged for my mother to have an abortion. My father,
who was informed after the fact, and who apparently never calcu-
lated the dates, talked to me about it a few times in later years. It
wasn't as if he would have tried to stop her, he said—and to this
day I don't know to what extent, if any, he heard his mind whispering something, and to what extent the years of drinking were
an attempt to drown it out—it was just that he couldn't understand
why she hadn't discussed it with him first. It was a decision they
should have made together.

And so, my father—the poor, unmanned sap who wouldn't
break the door down. Who couldn't understand that this gesture
was being asked of him because we repeat and repeat the things
that hurt us in the hope of making them our own. Who floundered
in that pit with my mother—a pit not of their making, which neither of them understood—most of his life.

Which brings me to my *dědeček,* my grandfather, the only one
of my grandparents that I ever met. For two weeks in 1963, in the
dead of winter, he visited us in Queens. I was five. I have a memory of walking with him down Queens Boulevard into a brutal
January wind, of running after him, terrified that he'd leave me
behind.

Even now, looking at his photograph, I want to reach down
into the frame and hit him before he can hurt me. It's not just
that he didn't smile—plenty of people don't smile, either because

they're sad, or shy, or because they don't see any humor in the world . . . my grandfather didn't smile because to smile would be to give you something—some recognition, some acceptance, something. He would give you nothing—because you wanted it, because you were weak. It gave him a certain small pleasure.

Let me put it this way: When I look at my grandfather's face—intelligent, self-contained, disapproving—I see a man standing by a cage with a starving dog. There's a bowl of food an inch or two beyond the reach of the dog's tongue. My grandfather doesn't move the bowl closer, nor does he push it further away—he just watches: Everything's perfect as it is.

How easy he makes it for me, with his Hitler mustache and his passion for order, shooting the neighbors' cats, then flinging their limp bodies into their owners' yards. It takes a certain kind of man, a certain kind of soul, not just to commit the act but feed on the hate it brings him, to fatten on it like a tick, just as it takes a certain kind of man to admire the murderers who have flooded his country, to align himself with them, to welcome the discipline they bring his people. It takes, in this case, nothing more than a petit bourgeois Czech bureaucrat with deep German roots. A man stamped in the SS mold.

The kind of man who would break down the door—but only if he knew he could hurt what was behind it.

XVII

A BALL BEARING, SUSPENDED on a string, slams into its brothers, and nothing happens. And then it does. So it is with us: Something happens—a mother unexpectedly walks into her daughter's room—and the trauma goes underground, vanishes . . . until it reappears, weeks or decades down the line.

It's a nice, writerly analogy—and a flawed one. I want to believe it, but I can't. Because we're not ball bearings. Because the laws of physics don't apply to the heart, or the mind, or to what used to be called the soul. They just don't. Newton can't help you here. Rhetorical tropes won't help you either—metaphors obscure as well as reveal.

Nothing about us is predictable, very little rational, nothing repeatable under identical conditions because identical conditions don't exist in the world of time. There's Heraclitus, dipping his toe in the river, then dipping it again. But it ain't the same river any more, and it ain't the same toe. How nice it would be if the energy of cruelty moved in a straight line, if the blow struck in 1945 erupted, on schedule, in 1963. Alas, because we're human, the bearing shatters into fragments, some of which may return to haunt us—where and when they damn well please—or not. Who knows how they'll visit? They can emerge in dreams. They can skip generations. They can be gone from this world—utterly gone—and reemerge in a slap, reborn in a cruelty that shocks the one who indulges it.

Only two things seem certain: that what we thought was the "featuring blow" was preceded by others that prepared the ground, and that one way or another, once that blow's been struck, we'll be making its acquaintance again. If there's anything immortal about us, it's the deeds we do. Acts are a form of energy; for better or worse—transformed, disguised—they go on forever.

In 1980, the year I graduated from college, my mother and I took a trip. A memorable one.

The journey across Europe from Rotterdam to Brno, billed as "our last trip as mother and son" (Why last? I kept wondering), was a quick descent—completely unexpected, shocking in its swiftness. By the first night in Rotterdam, where we would spend three rainy days in a tiny, dank pension with a nearly vertical staircase called the Van Der Hoot, she'd stopped talking, her face transformed into the haggard mask you see on those who've undergone some unfathomable grief, except that in this case the pain came larded with rage. The car, which my father had arranged to have sent from the Port of Newark, was late in arriving. He'd done it on purpose—stranded us here. She'd told him to see to this, arrange for that, warned him (in fact, she'd said nothing, left everything to him), and this is what it came to. It was always like this, always. I argued, tried to defend him, tried to make her feel better. She sat hunched on the bed under the low, tilted ceiling still wearing her raincoat, crying. No, it was always like this. Everything was like this.

I didn't know what to do. She wouldn't talk to me, wouldn't go out. For three days I'd leave her in the tiny room and walk all day through a city I didn't know, whose language I didn't speak, killing hours. On the fourth day, the car arrived.

She rallied, instantly optimistic. She put on some makeup and her Jackie Onassis sunglasses and we caught a taxi for the postapocalyptic wasteland of the Rotterdam shipyards, where "always" reasserted itself. We had a copy of the bill of lading, not the original; they couldn't release the car.

My mother broke down. She pleaded, then begged—actually begged—then wept, slumped in a chair in that little wooden office while I squatted next to her, my arm around her shoulders, embarrassed (to my retrospective shame), talking to her in Czech. God knows what I said. God knows what those Dutch office workers thought of this madness. Half an hour later, eager to be done with this mess that nobody had asked for, somebody signed off on the copy. Mom rallied, signed the release papers. The sunglasses came back on. We were off. It had worked, she said, backing out of the lot, it had all been an act, and not knowing what to say to something so obviously untrue—did she expect me to pretend to believe it? was this a test of some kind?—I played along, feeling as though I were somehow betraying her trust by agreeing with her. She'd fooled them alright, I'd never have guessed it, and she laughed as we merged onto a larger road—her hands gripping the wheel, her fingers stretching and flexing as though working out a cramp—while somewhere in my head a small, increasingly panicked voice was wondering what was happening, where this was going, and how soon—and how—I could get out.

From the outside, I suppose it could seem almost funny: We couldn't seem to get out of Rotterdam. Following the signs, we took exit after exit, merged and merged again . . . then recognized a landmark we'd passed twenty minutes or half an hour earlier. We tried it again, me helping to navigate with the map while reading signs, both of us agreeing that we'd seen what we'd seen: "It said right—it definitely said right." And there was the landmark—it had happened again. And then a third time.

The highways were fast, the drivers understandably impatient. A steady, misting rain blurred the traffic between swipes of the blades. My mother, scared now, was turning on me. I should find another route, she kept yelling. I couldn't see another route, I said—I had no idea where we were. Just look at the map, she screamed, find another route. Quick, was that a left? Did I see that? Quick—did it say left? Tell me what to do, quickly, quickly.

I'd been looking at the map, I said, I hadn't seen the sign.

For God's sake, should I take the exit? Oh, God, he's not letting me in! Decide!

Mom, I was—

Decide!

Left—take the left.

And she'd swerve onto the ramp in an angry blare of horns and we'd be more lost than ever. It was my fault. What was wrong with me—did I want to get us both killed? I was doing this on purpose. I wanted to ruin everything. I always wanted to ruin everything. I was my father's son.

Never one to turn the other cheek, I fought back. I was doing everything I could. I had no idea where the hell we were. Why didn't she pull over and look at the goddamn map herself, or better yet, let me drive?

She screamed at me—betrayed, deserted, as she always knew she'd be, all along, by all of us, because I was a coward, just like my father—clutching the wheel like the collar of her enemy, merging left, then right, aimlessly now, refusing to pull over, refusing to let me drive, then—lowering her voice to the kind of hiss of disgust you might hear from someone cutting an infection out of their own arm—said to me what she wouldn't say again for eight years until I came to visit her in Brno, leaving my pregnant wife in Cambridge, Massachusetts, and she dug through my suitcase, painstakingly packed with shirts and pants she'd approve of, and pulled out a t-shirt I'd brought in case I had a chance to take a run:

This is what you'd bring? she whispered, disbelieving. This is what you'd bring—to spite me, to embarrass me? She was staring at me over the top of the t-shirt, which she was holding by the edges like something obscene. *Ty seš zlej*, she hissed, outraged, disbelieving, like a child that's been struck for no reason, or like a witness confronting the child's attacker, or maybe even the attacker himself, yet at the same time—this is important—both broken and indomitable, like Medea confronting Jason with the bodies of his children, paying back his betrayal a hundredfold: *Ty seš zlej*—You're evil—then louder, declaring it as truth, as fact: *Ty seš zlej*. Then screaming it: *Ty seš zlej, zlej, zlej!*

By the time of the t-shirt, I was more prepared, protected, able to see the insanity of calling your son evil for packing a t-shirt. Able to defend myself. Outside of Rotterdam, eight years earlier, all I remember was a sense of shock edging on terror, as though my mother had suddenly opened her mouth and begun mewing like a cat. No, I'm not, I said, because I wasn't, because even then I knew I'd never be, not intentionally, not in my heart. No, I'm not, I said to her, but I was too late; some small part of me—three percent of me? five?—swayed by her hatred, assumed the guilt for it. Justice has nothing to do with it, this part of me said. She's your mother. Why would she say this if, on some level, in ways you can't understand or don't want to see, it wasn't true?

But that part of me would bide its time, go deep, reveal itself through the years in amusing ways; at the time, the part of me she'd raised fought back. I clung to truth, to reason, to sanity itself, refusing to budge, to move a single inch toward whatever place she'd found herself in, where she was fighting to the death surrounded by enemies, by hate, by evil itself.

How long this went on, I don't know. How we managed not to die on the autobahn that day is also a mystery—testimony to sheer luck or my mother's driving, probably the former. All I know is that it went on and on—that we fought as only she and I could fight, with me dug in, prepared to maintain my stand till the last dog died and her battering herself against my defenses, accusing, despising, belittling—and then we were somehow on the road to Germany, and my mother, screaming and weeping, deaccelerating from 140 kilometers an hour in the fast lane, was steering onto the median. The cement curb was low, we didn't bounce into traffic, we didn't roll; the car just plowed out onto the grass and stopped, the traffic blurring by on either side.

And there we sat. My mother wouldn't talk. She wept, the tears running from under the sunglasses she was wearing despite the clouds, the rain. I tried to reason with her, calm her. I wasn't a liar, I said—somehow, not being able to get out of Rotterdam had made me a liar—it wasn't my fault. It wasn't anybody's fault. It was OK. I asked if I could drive.

She didn't move. I was a liar. She'd said this, said that, warned me about such and such an exit. What had I done? I'd sneered at her, *ušklíbl se*—a kind of condescending, taunting sneer. No I hadn't, I said. She could remember precisely when it happened, how I'd looked, how I'd turned and said . . .

I asked if I could drive, get us out of there. She didn't move. I was a liar, not even man enough to admit when I was at fault. And so it went.

I don't honestly know how it was possible for us to sit there in the middle of that highway—maybe the entire Dutch police force had the day off, or maybe they recognized the Corolla with the American plates for the black hole that it was and wisely held back—but we did. We sat there for almost two and a half hours. I know because I looked. Two and a half hours is a long time to fight. For two and a half hours she wept and raged while the rain pounded on the roof and the traffic passed on either side of us trailing water like smoke. She wouldn't drive, and she wouldn't let me drive. By three a rainy dusk had set in.

I remember that afternoon as one of the most surreal in my life. I had no idea what to do. When this would end, or how. I couldn't wrestle the car away from her. I couldn't get out and start walking back to Rotterdam in the rain. Where would I go? I had no money. I couldn't reason with her, couldn't win; she'd built the story of my guilt, my treachery, so high that it had become real to her—absolutely, heartbreakingly, infuriatingly real. A fact. I might as well have been trying to convince her that we weren't in a car, or that it wasn't raining and hadn't rained in weeks.

Looking back, I think it was this ability to believe so completely in something of her own making—something that never was—to construct a narrative out of air, support it with made-up memories, then commit to it as though it represented the last measure of justice, that still amazes and appalls me. You could see it growing, beginning with the first small brick—the expression on my face, let's say, that particular thing I'd (never) said—then quickly cementing, gathering reality to itself, becoming indisputable, then fact. In some sense, my mother was like a method actor who is able to vanish into the scene—not *feel* grief or rage but actually grieve, rage—except that in her case the play never closed. My crime was real now, as real as anything in her life—it was the nail on which her sanity hung. For me to say that nothing had happened, or that she'd made it up for reasons of her own, was a metaphysical assault, as absurd as it was cruel.

I caved. I gave in. I was sorry, I said, still trying to salvage something with the usual qualifications: I was sorry she saw it that way. I hadn't meant, I hadn't intended. If it was my fault, I was sorry, though I didn't remember . . .

Meant, intended, if, though—none of these would do. Truth was truth. And sitting in that steamed up little car in the median of that highway heading toward the German border, utterly exhausted, just wanting to go, to find a place, to sleep, I gave her the truth she wanted. After all my denials, her respect for me ticked up a notch; at least I'd been man enough to admit my fault.

And she wiped herself a little window over the steering wheel with her handkerchief, checked her mirrors, and we bumped out onto the road to Germany.

XVIII

WHEN PEOPLE SOMETIMES ASK me about writing, I tell them that our books write us. It's not a particularly clever line, but I think it's true. The act of writing will reveal you, word by word, line by line. You can remain ignorant yourself, you can hide in the shrubbery of your prose till the day you die; to a great reader, you'll stand naked as the day.

I'm not a great reader, particularly of my own work. It's the reason I've been surprised by what my own books conspired to say behind my back. And not always pleasantly surprised. Sometimes I think it takes more guts to read what you've written than to write it in the first place.

In my third novel, *Brewster*, which showed my own childhood in the dark carnival mirror of fiction—stretching some parts, shrinking others—I never realized that by having my narrator lose his younger brother in childhood, I'd worked out the essential dynamic of my life. In *Brewster*, the narrator's immigrant mother, perpetually mourning the death of her idealized firstborn child, can't see the younger brother—even hates him for surviving. In my own life, my mother mourned the perfect child I'd once been, then turned on the pimpled traitor who'd survived. I spent three decades arguing on my behalf, saying, "I'm right here. I'm your son. Nothing's changed."

Obvious? Not to me. I was in the shower, four months after the book's publication, when I had my little epiphany. I remember standing there like a fool, soap in my armpits and egg on my face, suddenly aware of what had been hidden in plain view.

There were other times. I thought that "Dog," a story I wrote in the fall of 2007, was a deeply strange—all right, fucked-up— story about a man and his dog. The man loves his dog as the dog loves him. They're a church of two. They hang out together, play together, watch TV together. *And sliding down to sleep on the trough and crest of her breathing, he'd know that this was love, love as profound and true as the slowing of blood when the season's screw starts to tighten.* Just so.

Everything is daffodils and sunsets until the day the man finds a razor blade growing out of the dog's hide. He doesn't understand how this is possible, but there it is; the next day there are more. Soon the dog's a clicking mass of blades. They don't hurt her, but every time the man touches her—as she expects him to, because she loves him—he bleeds.

My God, is there anything more embarrassing than self-analysis through literature? Let the defense go out for a smoke and the prosecution proceed; behold the evidence of my obtuseness:

Exhibit A: *What hurt him most was her inability (or unwillingness) to understand, to insist on having her feelings hurt, to see his attempts to protect himself as a kind of betrayal. He understood why she felt this way, of course. She loved him unconditionally. . . .*

Exhibit B: *She would attack death itself for him without a moment's hesitation, and yet here she was, suffering . . . unable to comprehend why she'd been abandoned. Why he no longer loved her.*

Exhibit C: *The pills were from Mexico, a bright canary yellow. He pressed three into a piece of hamburger meat he'd brought in a plastic bag and walked over to the mound of blankets. He was already weeping when she began to lick his bleeding hand, working her tongue between his fingers. . . . Letting her lick the grease off his hand with her cut tongue, he jumped down into the grave and then, lifting her in his arms, laid her gently on the ground. There was plenty of room. Lying down beside her, he drew one of the blankets partly over himself and looked up at the rectangle of branches and sky. He'd taken eight himself; there was nothing else to do. He could feel her next to him, the slowing bellows of the lungs, the shallowing crest and trough of her breathing. "Good dog," he said. "Good dog."*

I missed it all. My mother? Don't be ridiculous—what did this have to do with my mother? In early drafts of the story, I'd made the dog male—some last feeble attempt on the part of my brain to hide from itself. Even after my agent suggested the switch, and I sensed the rightness of it, I *still* didn't make the link . . . until I did, and then it was like finding the hidden rake or badger or watering can in the picture in the dentist's office: I kept looking at it, wondering "How could I not have seen that?"

During the American Civil War, observers noted a curious fact: the sounds of a battle, clearly distinguishable at ten miles, could be utterly inaudible at two. These weird wrinkles in the landscape were called "acoustic shadows."

Maybe it's the same thing with memory, except that our inability to hear something in our past is proportional to the misery of the event; the uglier the battlefield, the deeper the shadow.

When I was eight or nine, I was in my room half-listening to my parents fight when a sound unlike anything I'd ever heard before—a kind of horrible, bellowing wail—rose from my father's study. I rushed into the hallway just in time to glimpse him lying on his stomach next to the metal filing cabinets, hitting his arms and legs against the floor like a giant infant, and then my mother's body blocked my view. And the memory vanished into shadow.

Perhaps ten years later, in college now, I had a profoundly erotic dream in which a vague but deeply desirable woman sat on a high stone wall looking down at me, wanting me. There were no edges to the dream, no borders—just the wall, the woman, and pale, yellow light. A rival appeared next to me, a man so huge he seemed more god than mortal—larger than life, impossibly powerful; he could reach the woman with ease. This made me angry and I pointed at him and he began to shrink, and I kept pointing, thrilled at my own power, until he was an infant at my feet, lying on his stomach, helpless kicking his arms and legs.

If I ever get therapy, I'll save that one for a special occasion—a treat for the holidays.

My point is that the original event—my father's breakdown—

remained hidden. It would be another fifteen years, until after he'd suffered a massive heart attack, until after I'd slept in the waiting room of the IC unit in Bethlehem for two nights wrapped in my coat, until I'd seen his morphine-bloated body hooked to a dozen machines that beeped and pulsed while he dreamed away in his coma, that the silence cracked, the hour returned, and there I was, nine years old again, glimpsing Daddy wailing on the floor. Go figure.

Truth makes you hungry for more truth. It's a bit like confessing—once you start, it's hard to stop. The trick is recognizing when truth-telling shades into self-indulgence, or worse, step-right-up exhibitionism.

I'm clearing my throat, stalling. If there's something unpleasant you need to do, we always told our kids—best get to it.

The thing is—I missed the cats. They were everywhere, a kind of go-to metaphor. I saw them, used them, but I didn't understand where they came from. Now that I do, I can see why I might not have wanted to know.

I can look almost anywhere now, and there they are. In my first novel, *God's Fool*, my nineteenth-century heroes wake late in the night to a strange, barking sound, and find a cat drowning in a well. In an essay on the virtues of idleness I claim that "we're moving product, while the soul drowns like a cat in a well." At the beginning of this memoir, for Christ's sake—the irony here is priceless—I imagine my subconscious daring me to ignore my past: "You want to strike out like the American Adam with your freeze-dried beef stroganoff and your telescoping walking stick? You want to fucking baptize yourself? Well good luck and God bless—I'll drown you like a cat in a well."

But I need to say something. Of all the animals I've loved in my life—and I'm the kind of person who rescues damsel flies from the lake, carries hatchling turtles off the roads in spring—I've probably loved cats the most. When Bob, who I loved ridiculously, disappeared two years ago—I missed him profoundly. I still do. Cruelty to animals makes me crazy—as does any cruelty, actually. I'd take a stick to Michael Vick in a heartbeat.

Time to connect the dots—or try.

My grandfather, the Nazi sympathizer, the man who most likely slept with his own daughter for years (because a man doesn't begin having sex with his daughter when she's nineteen, because it takes time to build that horror into habit)—this man, as I've said, also killed cats. An atrocity barely worth mentioning given his other sins, but revealing nonetheless. He did it regularly. He did it for years. He shrugged off the threats, the hate, accepted his ostracism philosophically.

I don't know when I learned this fact about Grandpa—not till my teens, probably.

In 1994, a father now, I woke up in our bedroom in Leucadia, California, to a weird, barking sound. It wouldn't stop. It was quite dark—perhaps an hour before dawn. Eventually, unable to sleep, I got dressed and went out back behind our apartment complex, then pushed aside the board in the fence that led to our garden. The strange, rhythmic barking was louder. Eventually, in a neighbor's yard in a cistern half full of water like a deep bathtub, my flashlight found a cat, barely swimming, barking desperately. I pried the board off the fence, levered the poor thing—soaked and small as a rat—out of the hole, carried it back to our apartment, where my wife wrapped it in towels, then drove it to a twenty-four-hour pet clinic in Carlsbad. We heard later it had to be put down. *Like a cat in a well*.

It troubled me deeply—if only I'd gotten up sooner—but I was still in the shadow of the larger thing.

I'd stay there another twenty years, through my thirties and forties and late into my fifties, until I traveled to see my mother in a care home for Alzheimer's patients in Brno. And I remembered. It was after we'd returned home to the States. I was driving somewhere with my wife, and suddenly I was telling her the story—as though I'd always known it, always remembered it. Just like that.

In the summer of 1977, my parents left for Europe—my father had some kind of work there. I was left in charge of our house in Bethlehem, Pennsylvania. I was nineteen. I could handle whatever needed handling, my mother said.

A week or two after they left, our cat, Chiquita, had a litter of kittens. It was her sixth, maybe her seventh. I don't know why we'd never had her fixed—it was less common then, or maybe we were just idiots. In any case, we hadn't. At regular intervals, a litter would arrive and I'd spend days giving kittens away to strangers, to pet stores, to anyone who would take them.

But I was a man now, and I knew what a man would do because I'd been told. In the Old World, you see, in the old days, the country people were a tough, practical lot; if a cat had a litter, they'd put the kittens in a bag with a rock—*do pitlu s kamenem*—and throw them in the river. It was hard but necessary—otherwise the country would be overrun. And if you did it right away, while they were still blind and small, it went very quickly.

My father hated doing it, but he had, once or twice, returning from the garage white and sick in the face, unable to talk. But he was my father, and though part of me felt sorry for him, well, he wasn't Steve McQueen. And I was a man now. I did due diligence, tried to place them, made a few calls. No one wanted kittens, nor were they likely to. I got a bucket, filled it with water. I almost relished the responsibility, the chance to show I could do the hard thing. Hell, I couldn't have my parents return to a house full of cats. And besides, if I did it right away, while they were still blind and small, it would go very quickly.

It did not go very quickly. I can't go into the details—I won't. Perhaps there were some air pockets in the bag. Impossibly, I could hear their miniature mewling all through the house. I couldn't get away from it. It went on and on. I was horrified by what I'd done, too scared to get them out, thinking I'd find them half-gone, dying. . . . I wasn't a man—I wasn't even my father. I was a child, wiping away tears, swallowing down the taste of my own vomit. . . .

To this day, I think it may be the most despicable thing I've done—the thing I'm most ashamed of. Was it Mommy's fault, or Steve McQueen's? Sorry—that's a coward's out I won't take. It was mine, and to say that it went against my nature, or that for those three or four minutes I existed in the most profound state of self-revulsion I've known, doesn't alleviate my guilt; it compounds it.

Why? I can tell you why: Because I didn't stop. Because I made myself do the hard thing even though it made me sick; because, for all I know, most of the terrible things done in this world are difficult for the people who do them, are, in fact, a violence against the self.

You tell me it went against your nature? I don't care. That it was hard? I don't care. That it gave you pain to do this thing—that it still gives you pain? You'll get no mercy from me.

It's impossible for me to deny it. For just those few minutes, in my own small way—though I'm not for a moment comparing our deeds—I came within range of my grandfather's gravitational pull, sensed in myself the seed of his cruelty, and I'll spend my life trying to uproot it.

XIX

THE SPRING OF 1945 WAS, or should have been, a time of reckoning with what our species is capable of. Over the previous six years, 50 million souls had disappeared into a furnace so profound it would wither any attempts to reckon its magnitude, caking the brain, leaving only a still, annealing dust for which there could be no analogies, no accounting, out of which we could draw no saving truth. All that remained were apparent facts, recorded dates, accounts of events and motivations so jarring, so emotionally dissonant that they seemed to refer to some other world, a realm from which both humanity and sense had been surgically removed.

I grew up in the shadow of this time; in our house, 1945 never really ended. Drawn like a moth to our contradictions, hypnotized by the damned human race, I couldn't help but dwell—and wonder.

During the last days of the Third Reich, for example, as the concussions of the Russian heavy artillery jingled the crystal in the cabinets of the Reichschancellery in Berlin, Propaganda Minister Goebbels would while away the long after-dinner hours reading to Hitler from Thomas Carlyle's history of Frederick the

Great. I could see it: Hitler, perhaps, at one end of a plum-colored damask sofa, his head leaning on his right hand, absentmindedly running his middle finger along the center of his brow; Goebbels in a comfortable chair opposite, one leg draped over the other, a fire companionably puffing and spitting . . .

And there, in one of the well-furnished rooms of the armor-plated, concrete-reinforced bunker beneath the Chancellery (only six years after passing through the line of sight of a fifteen-year-old boy standing behind a thick, blue curtain), Adolf Hitler wept, touched by Carlyle's apostrophe to the long-dead king in the moment of his greatest trial: "Brave King! Wait yet a little while, and the days of your suffering will be over. Already the sun of your good fortune stands behind the clouds and soon will rise upon you."

Sixty feet over their heads, the nine-hundred-room Chancellery, with its polished marble halls and hundred-pound chandeliers, was methodically being pounded into dust and rubble: stacks and columns of books taken from the Chancellery libraries blocked the tall windows looking out onto the wrecked Wilhelm-strasse, the short, ugly barrels of machine guns poking between the spines; bulky crates of crosses and oak leaves barricaded the main entrance. A month earlier, Anglo-American armies had crossed the Rhine.

None of this mattered. Sensing a promise, an omen of redemption in Carlyle's description of Frederick's deliverance, Hitler sent a guard to retrieve the Reich's official horoscopes. And there it was: proof that, just as Prussia had been saved in the darkest hours of the Seven Years' War by the miraculous death of the czarina, so the Third Reich would survive her harshest trials. History would save her. "Even in this very year, a change of fortune shall come," Goebbels proclaimed in an eleventh-hour message to the retreating troops. "The Führer knows the exact hour of its arrival. Destiny has sent us this man so that we . . . [can] testify to the miracle. . . ."

A few days later, Goebbels had his miracle, his czarina. Returning to Berlin late on the night of April 12, the capital around him rising in flames, he was approached by a secretary with urgent news: Franklin Roosevelt was dead. Phoning the news to Hitler in the bunker beneath the burning Chancellery, Goebbels was ecstatic. Here, blazingly revealed at last, was the power of Historical Necessity and Justice. The news, he felt, would revive the spirit of the German people. His feelings seem to have been shared by most of the German Supreme Command. "This," wrote Finance Minister Schwerin von Krosigk in his diary, "was the Angel of History! We felt its wings flutter through the room."

Less than two weeks later, in the cramped air-raid shelter of the Ministry of the People's Enlightenment and Propaganda, Goebbels's six children lay dead, their lips, eyes, arms and legs turned blue from the potassium cyanide pills given to them by their father. Goebbels's wife, Magda, who had apparently dressed the children for the occasion, was also dead, shot by her husband, who then poured gasoline on her and set fire to her skirt. Goebbels himself, after killing his family, poured gasoline on his clothes, set fire to a trouser leg, then turned the gun to his temple. Across the Wilhelmplatz, German gunners lay buried beneath the crumbled barricades of books, the high-ceilinged rooms behind them wavering in the heat of raging fires. In a small room in the bunker below, having rejected poison after watching the agonized deaths of the Chancellery dogs, Adolf Hitler sat down on a deep-cushioned brocade sofa next to the body of his bride, Eva Braun, put a gun in his mouth, and pulled the trigger. Blood flowed down and coagulated on the brocade. The Angel of History fluttered its wings.

I can see von Krosigk's angel, inscrutable as any mortal, clattering like a CGI fairy over my diorama of the city of Brno, sowing fire or favor as the mood grabs him, linking small things to large, indulging his taste for whimsy. It's as good a way as any of explaining how, thirty-four years after Adolf Hitler shot himself on that brocaded sofa, forty years after my father watched his motorcade pass through Brno, I found myself in an apartment on West 69th Street in New York holding a bloodstained piece of cloth that had been cut out of that same sofa by a young journalist named Beatrix Turner who'd talked her way into the bunker on May 4, 1945, cut out a souvenir, and who now, four decades later, wanted to prove to the skeptical college kid helping her out in her old age that it had all been true.

Of course it's pure egotism, this business of linking our lives to Big History, of drawing connections between things so vastly different in magnitude, but who can resist it? The blurring of years and fates brings a sense of weightlessness, of grandeur, of historical vertigo.

It's 1939. My fifteen-year-old father watches Hitler's motorcade come through Brno. I don't exist; I'll be resting in the other dark another nineteen years.

It's 1945. The same man my father saw from his window puts a gun in his mouth and pulls the trigger with his thumb. As the hammer hits, a journalist named Beatrix Turner is already making her way across the rubble of Berlin toward the Reichschancellery, where she'll talk and flirt her way past the Russian guards, grope her way down the flooded stairs in the dark and cut herself a souvenir stained with his blood.

It's 1979. Suddenly in her frail seventies, Beatrix Turner hires a broke and impatient college student named Slouka (is it Mike?) to clean her apartment and sign her checks and ends up convincing him that she is who she is and did what she did by digging a cloth stained with Hitler's blood out of her closet.

It's 1997. My sixteen-year-old father is an old man now; I'm married with children. Over lunch with my editor at *Harper's Magazine*, I tell him the story of Beatrix Turner and Hitler's couch. He commissions an essay on the spot, I write it, and *Harper's* (after asking me to present my journal from 1979 to the magazine's fact-checkers) pays my rent for slightly less than two months. I send the essay to my father, who likes it, but tells me the curtains he looked through sixty years earlier were red, not blue.

"What's the takeaway?" my neighbor's always asking his kids whenever they run into something harder than they are. It's a good question. I suppose the takeaway is that we live in history the way fish live in water. Whether we know it or not. Care or not. Whether the "fact-checkers" give us their stamp of approval—or not. We're of it. Our dance in the current doesn't have to yield a meaning. It doesn't have to be significant. Our time will braid with others'—helplessly.

Significance is in the eye of the beholder. For me, what matters is not some tortured connection I might make between the fact that Adolf Hitler committed suicide the same month—the same hour, for all I know—that my grandmother walked into my mother's room to find her husband (with his Hitler mustache) with her daughter, but the fact that neither event was quite the ending it seemed to be.

The *ongoingness* of things fascinates me. It connects Big History to small, our lives to our stories. It's my one Truth, which I sing with the zeal of the converted: Life runs through the finish line; the period is just a comma in embryo. To wit: Adolf Hitler blows his brains out and the war echoes on, shaping actions and attitudes for generations to come. My mother escapes her house and the nightmare comes with her. You think it's a new beginning? It's not.

Nothing dies, and that's both good and bad.

I wish I could have warned them. Sat them down in some café the week before the wedding and said, "For God's sake, don't be fooled—whatever the opposite of a beginning is (without actually being an end) this is it. Your one chance is to drag this thing between you out of the shadows, expose it mercilessly, beat that fucker to death with words before it tunnels into your souls—and if you think I'm being melodramatic, I am, but not nearly enough."

But I wasn't around yet, and so they danced their dance and now they're gone—from this life, or, in my mother's case, from everything that gives life meaning. And that, as they say, is that.

And yet.

XX

IF I STAND BACK far enough—the moon might do it—I can almost see some humor in it: "So Olinka and Zdenek are getting married! How lovely! What a handsome couple they'll make. Of course, like all newlyweds, they'll have the usual wrinkles to iron out: the blushing bride's abortion of her father's child, for one, and the troublesome fact that the rapist lives, unpunished, unrepentant, a tram ride away. And then there's the bridegroom's utter cluelessness— an obtuseness, an innocence so profound, so fated, so downright Greek, it requires a willing suspension of disbelief to believe at all— and, finally, adding a wash of Big History to this private horror, the fact that the country they live in is still spasming after six years of war, gasping for air like a swimmer about to be buried again . . . but hey, what are these things compared to Love?"

I realize the race is never even, the handicaps never fair. But this? This feels gratuitous, rigged. This is like toeing the starting line for a race and having the starter say: "On your marks, set— by the way, you there, second from the left, I tied your ankle to a truck—go!"

It's only when I allow myself to see them as they were then that it gets me. In the spring of 1945 my dad was not yet twenty-two; my mother, nineteen. They were good kids. What chance did they have? I see them setting up their little apartment, playing husband and wife, and the sadness is almost unbearable.

They had a June wedding, God help me. A quick, minimal thing. I don't know who was present. I can't imagine anything more freighted than their wedding night, more unfair to them both.

The new marriage didn't set—a shock, I know. Within a month, my father, a reporter at *Lidové Noviny,* began staying late at the office, ignoring his bride, returning home at midnight, then at one in the morning, then two. My mother, so the story goes, didn't know what was wrong, how she was failing him, what to do. She couldn't ask her mother's advice because, well, good Catholic girls didn't talk about such things with their mothers in those days. And so, neglected, alone, watching the dinner she'd made congealing on the table, she began starving herself.

This is what she told me and I didn't think to question it: Of course she starved herself—she was unhappy. I'd be in my fifties—such is the staying power of the things we're told when we're young—before it occurred to me that starvation is probably not the most normal response to marital discord. That something else might have been involved.

Still, as Exhibit A in the case of *Mommy's Pain v. Daddy's Callousness,* this was powerful stuff: As his bride was starving, Dad was yukking it up at the office, knocking out copy, busily ignoring the disaster.

That the picture doesn't square with the man I knew doesn't change the fact that my mother did, in fact, almost succeed in killing herself. She wasn't fucking around. Within six months she'd withered down to forty-five kilos—about a hundred pounds. By the spring of 1946 she was down to forty-one. He didn't know what to do, my father told me fifty years later. Of course he knew something was terribly wrong. Almost from the beginning, it was as if she didn't want to be with him. He didn't know where to turn. Desperate, he eventually asked her mother, who advised him to be more attentive. He thought there was something wrong with him. That it was his fault somehow. And so, yes, it was true—he hid in his work.

There were terrible fights, many of them growing from the smallest misunderstandings as if fueled by some hidden grievance. They changed nothing. *For in tremendous extremities human souls are like drowning men.* In nine months my mother had shrunk into a premonition of the skeleton I'd find sixty-nine years later in a care home just two miles away.

What compels us to hurt ourselves is hardly ever this obvious: Every Saturday that first year, my mother and father would board the tram with a basket of whatever food they'd been able to find and go visit my mother's parents, where my mother would find what had happened to her buried so neatly that the thing itself, still breathing under the smiles and the small talk, began to seem false—a ghastly invention of her own making.

Half of her wanted nothing more than to believe it was just that. The other half, holding fast to a truth that burned her, fought against letting go as if fighting for life itself. An existential rack—I can't think of anything crueler.

And so, forced to endure the weekly ritual—the kisses on the cheek, the compliments on the little sandwiches, or chlebíčky, forced to literally break bread with her abuser-father as her husband sat by, uncomprehending—my mother began to turn on herself; the mind, in its magnificently unjust way, exacted its price . . . and charged the body. Whether she understood what was happening or not, I don't know. It didn't matter. *Well enough they know they are in peril; well enough they know the cause of that peril; yet the sea is the sea, and these drowning men do drown.*

Or twenty-year-old girls, as the case may be.

Except when they don't. Told by her doctor that she was months away from major organ failure if something didn't change, my mother somehow dragged up the will to apply for a summer job in a language camp in the forests of Moravia. She'd always loved languages.

She got the job, packed and left. It must have taken enormous strength to wrench herself out of that slide, but then my mother always had a gift for the violent gesture—the hurled peach, the lunge for the sapling. She'd go hard, make it difficult, get in her own way. She'd fight herself to a standstill.

My mother left Brno (and her first life) on a hot Sunday morning. She had one small suitcase.

I can see her on that day, fragile as an insect, making her slow way down the shadow side of the platform, climbing aboard the 9:52 to the town of Žďár nad Sázavou with the help of an elderly conductor whose nose is as delicately blue-veined as a piece of Stilton. Two hours ahead, the man who will fill her heart for the next thirty years pours himself a second cup of coffee, then walks through the shade of the courtyard to meet his first class.

Even now I'm tempted to rewrite it—to make what actually happened more believable by making it less true—but I already did that once.

XXI

MAYBE NOW AND THEN the powers that be, bored of watching us get run through by invisible things, stifle a yawn and say, "Enough for now. Let's try something different, shall we?" And just like that, love's cavalry comes thundering in.

I can't explain it. I don't know that I have to.

I like to think of them that morning, the dotted lines of their fates converging; it gives me pleasure to imagine their ignorance of what lies ahead. "Just wait," I want to say to them, like a parent placing a gift under the tree—"You have no idea."

I picture my mother, a third my age, looking out the train window that hot morning at the passing barley fields, the blood-drops of poppies, at the slate-roofed villages with their cluttered little gardens—a metal wheelbarrow lying on its side on a pile of bricks, the gray cloth of a spillway in the shade, the winking of a water wheel. I imagine F. lying under the sheets with his hands locked behind his head trying to recall the dream he had, then sitting up and moving aside the curtains to see what kind of day it will be.

If I could say something to them now—if I could be in that train compartment with her, or standing by the coffee pot in the cafeteria—what would I say? Would I give them my blessing, say, "Go, go and don't look back," or would I say, "Wait, save yourself"— because, really, what were the odds that love could outrun its own decline?

The train sways on. The village, the garden, the small gray cloth of the spillway pass. The curtain drops. And the dotted lines converge.

XXII

My mother knew a man during the war. Theirs was a love story, and like any good love story, it left blood on the floor and wreckage in its wake.

I tried to write them once before; I've been writing her all my life.

The words are from a novel, *The Visible World*, specifically from a section that I called "A Memoir" because the amount of fact I'd poured into it had tipped the story into something other than fiction. I wouldn't say "more." Other.

A memoir embedded in a novel; an apt description of my life.

Looking back, I see that I stretched and pulled their story because it was too much for me then, too vast a canvas, and because I thought no one would believe it if I wrote it straight. Fiction would allow me to shape the deeper truth. This is what I told myself. Maybe it's true.

But I'm older now, my mother's gone, and I'm less concerned with being believed. It's time to settle up with memory, square what can be squared, come to terms.

XXIII

I DON'T KNOW WHERE love goes when we die, but more than most things, it's hard for me to believe in its passing.

My mother's love for the man I'll call F. was a big love, unstoppable, and if it left blood on the floor and wreckage in its wake, well, that's all right. The blood was their own, mostly, and love that matters can be messy.

They didn't know each other during the war. They met a year later, in a language camp in the forests of Moravia. In summer. She was skeletal, twenty, "fixin' to die" as the song says; he was a year younger, a Green Beret during the war, now a teacher of Spanish.

And then there's the one of him. I've looked at it closely. At the overlong sleeves of the sweater—the left pushed partway to the elbow, the other almost covering his hand. I've studied the cigarette, like a tiny stub of light clamped between the tips of his fingers, protruding from inside the wool. There's nothing to see. A man standing in the snow, squinting into the glare. Not particularly handsome. The snow behind him has partly melted.

Well, no—sorry. I didn't have the actual photograph at the time I described it in *The Visible World*; I had to remember it, and recollection is fiction.

I found the actual photograph last summer, curled like a leaf on the table next to my mother's bed in the boarded-up bedroom in which she spent the last years of her life before being moved to the care home. And there, painfully obvious, were the lines of my embroidery: no sweater, no cigarette stub, no sleeve pushed partway to the elbow. What I remembered as "partly melted snow" was actually a long, cerrated shadow cast by a row of pines.

Not particularly handsome? Hard to say. Handsome enough, I think. He's standing in a snowy cut between the pines, a pair of skis on his shoulder, his right hand resting on his hip. He's wearing some kind of open, military-style jacket, a thick scarf at the neck; his dark hair, combed straight back, is starting to recede. He's squinting into the sun—I got one thing right—and there's something about the way he's standing, the hand on the hip, even the squint, that conveys a certain kind of easy masculinity, a confidence in his place in the world that was still there almost thirty years later, when I met him.

But I'm getting ahead of myself. In the summer of 1946, the Spanish teacher and the English teacher saw each other and fell in love. For life, as far as I know. What she saw in him seems obvious enough. What he could have seen in her—shockingly thin, trembling with fatigue, husbanding her energy like a woman in her seventies—is anybody's guess. There was nothing of the savior about him, no apparent need to be a port in the storm for anybody, so my guess is that what he saw in her was her strength. And what he saw, she became. She started eating, she put on weight; she blossomed like the proverbial rose.

It must have been quite a thing, that stolen season. With its hidden ponds and its silent, moss-furred woods, there are few places more romantic in the summer than the forests of Moravia; for six weeks my mother and F. (whose initials she would write on the back of his photograph when her mind began to go), stole every hour they could, quietly coordinating their schedules for common mornings or afternoons off, then going in separate directions, one with a bit of bread and cheese, the other a blanket. . . .

To say it was an infatuation, a current too insistent to resist, is not enough. It was, by all accounts, mutual, overwhelming, joyous, insatiable. But it was more than that. These two people—and the miracle is that they knew it—were meant to be together. This was a big love.

And then she told him, or it slipped out somehow. She was married.

The shock, the anger, even, was predictable: Why hadn't she told him? Why had she hidden this from him? What did she think would happen? She'd meant to tell him, she explained. It was just that it had all happened so fast, and once the right time had passed, it became harder and harder to make things right.

He broke it off. I can't blame him. Raised Roman Catholic and dirt poor, his notion of adventures—of which he'd had his share—did not include affairs with married women. Even worse, in some ways, was the sudden uncertainty: What did he mean to her? What *could* he mean to her? And what the hell was he supposed to do now? In a few days she'd be returning to Brno, to her husband, sleeping in another man's bed.

If they broke up, and I seem to remember they did, each going their separate way—she in tears, he devastated—it didn't last long. Or, at any rate, didn't last. How often they actually saw each other over the next two years before my parents' escape across the border, I don't know. I don't know if they spoke of the future, or talked themselves into knots the way lovers who can't be together tend to do.

What I do know is that they'd both seen the face in the crowd that defines you—the face, the voice, that no cynicism can undercut; the one that says, "You're home, you're safe—now shut the door." That's one thing I do know. The other is that my mother, a Roman Catholic herself, was married. In short, a hopeless situation made endurable, but only just, by youth, which doesn't do hopeless.

A purgatory of hope, of waiting for some unforeseen thing to change. When I imagine my mother and F. in 1946 and '47, hanging on to their love, I see Kafka's petitioner before the door to the Law. In the famous parable from *The Trial* he waits for months, then years, then decades; he grows old and deaf. He doesn't understand why he's not allowed to enter—the Law should be for everyone, he feels. He pleads and argues with the guard, petitions for entrance, and always the answer is the same: Entrance is impossible—now.

Eventually, dying, he whispers his last question into the guard's hairy ear: Why was he denied entrance?

"Because this door was made specifically for you," the guard bellows into the old man's ear: "I am now going to shut it."

If love is a kind of law, my mother and F. didn't have to wait that long. The world, which had a card to play, played it.

XXIV

WHAT CAN I SAY about my father that isn't bent out of truth by hindsight, misshapen by love? My father was a good and decent man, I think, a man capable of outrage over the world he happened to have found himself in, but someone whose faith in reason, like some men's faith in God, or love, remained intact long after his life had made it ridiculous. He couldn't help it. His every gesture departed from that well-lit station, and though he understood how quaint this was, he was powerless to change it. It was his nature, and he wore it with dignity, like a childhood hat one has long outgrown but can't remove for the rest of his life. And somehow I could never bring myself to hold it against him.

I've been sitting here a while now, watching the snow come down on Prospect Street, trying to square the fictional father with the man I knew and loved. And I just don't know. The portrait isn't wrong—my father *was* a good and decent man, I think—but it's not entirely right, either. Though he believed in reason, for example, his quintessentially Czech nose for absurdity complicated things, particularly as he got older. And though decent at heart, he was rarely that calm, that accepting of himself; he had his passions, his regrets—he flailed like the rest of us.

So what was my fictional father—named Antonin in the novel—all about? Was I creating a portrait of the man I wished my father to be, flattering myself by imagining someone whose faults didn't remind me of my own? Was I setting up an alternative DNA?

If that was the motivation—and I think it probably was—I failed us both. My father was neither that decent nor that resigned. Neither am I, and though I may become both with age, I doubt it. I've always been too much in the world, too involved, both in love with what *is* and at war with it. It's a complicated way to be—I can't recommend it—but I seem stuck with it. The idea of justice has something to do with it.

By 1945 the janitor's son had graduated high school, become an editor at *Lidové Noviny*, begun the lifelong project of proving himself to the grocers' sons and hairdressers' daughters who'd shunned him in the courtyard when he tried to play with them. It was a task he could never finish, not even when, years later, the janitor's kid would greet Václav Havel, the president of the Czech Republic, whose visit to the United States he'd largely arranged.

Nothing could fill that gap, nothing could be enough. They'd always be there—sneering, throwing clods, or worse, ignoring him. Deep down, he was always returning to that courtyard, a sixty-year-old man now, a full professor, to show them, to make them take it back, to get his measure of justice, but something would always happen as he walked down those four cracked steps to the narrow passage that led into the half-light of the courtyard: his skin would smooth, he'd shrink in size, the well-cut suit would fall away, and they'd laugh at him standing there with the tears cutting a path to the corners of his mouth, babbling some nonsense about the president—and in my dreams it would be me striding out of that passage, grabbing the little bastards by the scruff, showing them how completely worthless and cruel they were. . . .

How condescending a son's pity is—and how very much like love. And how misguided, possibly. Who's to say, were it possible for me to make my way back to that courtyard, that I wouldn't be rescuing him from the one thing that made him who he was, that enabled him to force the world's attention?

XXV

THERE ARE TIMES I think the past is nothing more than a room attached to ours. We enter it a hundred times a day, argue with whoever's there; we flatten a cowlick, move the vase, true the picture on the wall.

I recall standing at the window looking out at my garden some years ago (something I tend to do in November) and thinking of my father. For just one second it seemed impossible that he should be eighty-seven and living in Prague—where they were having an early winter, he said—while I found myself six time zones back, renting a house no more than five minutes from where we'd once lived as a family. It felt like I could just walk over, find us there.

A cat appeared on the fence and a gust of sparrows rose against the neighbors' house. My wife and I had cleared the beds the day before, hauling off long armloads of pea vines segmented like the legs of sea creatures; for the first time in months I could see the wooden borders framing the dirt.

Zdenek Slouka. When I say my father's name out loud, I hear his voice coming out of my mouth. Years ago I stopped using my middle name—his first. He never mentioned it. He remarried later, but it didn't matter: We were the only ones left, and we both knew it.

It's hard for me to see his life as anything but a column of subtractions, as if God, picking flowers for the celestial vase, decided out of curiosity to pluck one bare—he loves me, he loves me not. His parents, whom he had to leave behind when he escaped from Czechoslovakia in 1948, died before the regime that had exiled him fell. He never saw them again; I never met them. His sister, Luba, my only aunt, threw herself out of a window in 1950, though my father wouldn't know about it for two years, imagining her all that time walking to school or lying in the grass above the athletic stadium in Brno with her friends—a temporary afterlife, like an image in a bubble. When a letter finally got through in September of 1952, the knowledge that she'd been gone so long made for a grief both slightly uncanny and tinged by insincerity—like going under anesthesia, I imagine, watching your own leg being removed.

And so it went, leaf by leaf. An old friend, a Latinist reduced to doing manual labor for refusing to join the Party, sat down to dinner the day before Christmas, 1966, cracked a walnut and died. Eventually there were just the three of us: my father, my mother, and me. The nuclear unit, famously unstable.

Whatever the question, my mother, who he must have made love with at least once, was not the answer. Not for him. An only child herself (capable of the most spontaneous joy I've ever known in an adult), she was broken by sixty, battered by gusts of sadness and rage. When she finally divorced my father in 1991 after forty-six years of marriage, she moved, along with the uncomfortable suburban furniture that had filled our home, to a mold-ridden farmhouse in Moravia where she re-created the rooms she'd been so miserable in, then gradually forgot everything: our cabin at Lost Lake, the days we laughed, the hot afternoons at the station when we'd wait for my father in the burnt electric smell of the ties and the steel—everything. A mercy for someone infatuated with regret. "Zdenek? Zdenek who?" she asked me four years ago, still here but not.

Which left just my father and me to carry all that history. We carried it well enough those last years—my father especially. Wedded to reason, inclined like a heliotrope to whatever could be known (author of the monograph *The Intercontinental Shelf and International Law*), he had the gift of being able to accept the gavel coming down, of being able to bear the sentence: "It wasn't." The comma and the conjunction he left to me, the lord of revision: "It wasn't, but it could have been."

"It could have been." He must have sensed the gene in me long before I did. There I was, like an apprentice St. Sebastian, inserting my baby arrows into my skin, practicing. My mother's son. Time didn't lay down its tracks in a line for me, the print didn't set: I mourned every house before we'd left it, then refused to leave it after we had. *Was* meant nothing to me; long before I knew what the conditional mood was, I was humming its tune: *If he had known, if she had said, if we had stayed*. My life, my work, was one long argument for commutation.

My father had no ear for it. To traffic in "if" was absurd, an exercise in masochism. What was, was. His sister was gone, sent in a fit of delirium tremens on an errand through thin-paned glass to the courtyard three stories below. His mother, awakened by a sound she would never forget, was also gone. It was the way it was.

In December, 1948, the day he learned that he was to be arrested, my father quietly began making arrangements to escape his own country. It couldn't have been easy—he could tell no one. Those who knew him would be interrogated; their ignorance would need the ring of truth. He'd have to vanish with a wink and a wave, disappear out of their lives like a magician's assistant stepping into a wardrobe. The only thing making it bearable—a saving irony—was his certainty that he wouldn't be gone long: a year, maybe two. The regime could never last.

The afternoon before he left, my father told his mother and sister that he'd be going to see a friend in Prague after the late edition of the paper. He'd be back in Brno on Monday. He gave his mother a quick hug, careful not to raise her suspicions, kissed his sister on the forehead. His father was still at the office.

At eight o'clock that night my father walked out of the clatter and ring of carriage returns for a few minutes to wake himself up in the cold winter air and ran into his father coming home from work. The two men stopped to talk as the snow came down. He was going to Prague for a day or so, my father said.

He'd heard, my grandfather said, lighting a cigarette. Did he have everything he needed?

It was an odd question. Sure, my father said. He'd be staying with Mirek.

"Money?"

He was fine, my father said.

My grandfather nodded, then looked up the street at the cones of snow coming down from the lamps like light in a comic book. "So," he said, "I better be getting home, before your mother begins to wonder." He smiled (and I can imagine that smile, though fifty years have passed since he died, because I'm only two years younger than he was then): "You'd better get back in there—don't you have a newspaper to put out?" And he put out his hand and my father took it and then he was walking away up the sidewalk past the closed shops toward the square.

My father stood there until he couldn't see him any longer and went back to work. He would never see him again. He'd be sixty-eight before he returned, his own son ten years older than he himself had been when he left.

The day he told me about that evening we were sitting on the deck behind our house. Things had happened the way they did, he said, imparting the lesson, the attitude, as always. What was, was. So what if he'd known, if he'd held his father's hand a little longer, or given him a hug—he hadn't. He looked out over our yard, already figuring out what needed his attention. He could use my help in the garden.

It was 1978, summer. I was home from college. We were still a family—sort of. My mother still had a memory.

———————

Seventeen years later saw some changes. The revolution had swept in like a welcome tide, receded; the three of us had separated. My mother had returned to Moravia. My father was living in Prague by then, working in the Academy of Sciences on Národni Street, a cavernous, museum-like building with forty-foot ceilings and empty, unlit corridors. He'd stay late, working, reading, drinking, and I'd find him there, groping my way toward the flat European switches on the wall that lit another section of hallway, temporarily, then went out behind me.

It was there, in the Academy of Sciences Building, my father told me, that he experienced one of the oddest moments of his life.

He'd been working late, he said, when a knock on the door nearly stopped his heart. It was well after midnight; the building had been dark for five hours or more. My father opened the door to a man in his early forties carrying a small, battered briefcase. The man extended his hand and gave his name—the standard Czech greeting. "Zdenek Slouka," he said.

My father, naturally enough after all the years he'd lived in America, assumed the man had asked him his name instead of giving his own. "I'm Zdenek Slouka," he replied, "can I help you?" The man smiled—a kind, strangely familiar smile. "No, I know you're Zdenek Slouka," he said. "The thing is, so am I."

They talked nearly till dawn, and a story emerged—a story, my father said, that he would never have believed if he hadn't heard it himself. The other Zdenek Slouka had been conceived out of wedlock. He didn't remember his father, a man from Brno, who had quietly supported him through his childhood and who had asked, in return, that he be named Zdenek.

One by one, the pieces locked into place. The conclusion was obvious. The other Zdenek, my father told me, was from the same logging town that his father had originally come from, and to which he'd begun returning late in life. It was there that he'd had an affair, fathered a December child. And it was there, apparently, staggering under the erasure of his family—his daughter's suicide, his wife's slide into madness, his son's disappearance into exile—that he'd taken a stab at the impossible, a gesture at once absurd and bottomlessly sad. He began again. He fathered a son, then named him after the one he'd lost. The man in the office was not just his namesake, my father said, but his half-brother. In other words, my uncle.

We were sitting in a café on Londynská Street. My father signaled the waitress and pointed to his vodka. Of course the whole thing was mad, a testament to the things that pain can drive us to, no more. But the man was real enough. And it was a comfort, wasn't it?—knowing we had a relation in the world, a good man apparently, eager to know us both.

I lived with the thought of this man, this second father, for quite a few years. Though I never actually met him—he was always gone, or traveling, when I visited Prague—I'd hear about him from my father. He'd called from Vienna, he'd tell me; he was coming to town the week after next. Over time I heard less, forgot to ask. Gradually he faded, a photograph left in the development tray. It didn't matter. Fixed in my imagination, having elbowed a space for himself in the past, he lived on. It took a long time for me to admit that he'd probably never been.

It was the small things that turned the key: a date that didn't match, a part that didn't fit, even that overelaborate frame in which the thing had been set: the fateful knock at midnight, the long-lost brother, emerging out of the dark. . . . My father had been drinking then, weighing accounts. I can see him, sitting up late in the Academy of Sciences, working his way down the bottle. The rationalist, cornered at last. His own losses he could bear; my own—imagined or real—were another thing. I was his only son, the only child of only children—existentially alone in terms of blood—and he was getting old.

So he made me a gift. His father, forced to let his son go into the world alone, had had no choice. He did. I'd have a relation, a companion—someone to talk to in the long years of exile.

Regrets accrue, old investments come to term; I've never been able to laugh at the concessions that love can force from us.

But I don't think it was for me alone that my father bent his faith, that he tried, awkwardly, to walk into the past, to flatten a cowlick, adjust the vase, make it right; there was another consideration, a moment in the past, like a bone in the throat, that needed his attention. And I know what it was because now and then time leaves a marker—a note in the margin, a corner turned down—so that we know where to look.

December, 1948. It's snowing. They talk. My grandfather knows. He turns, walking quickly, the years lowering like an anvil. Fifty years later my father, unable to bear it, comes to his rescue: he stalls the descent, jams a story between iron and stone, delivers to him a second son.

XXVI

I HAVE A CONFESSION to make: The previous chapter appeared as an essay in 2011, the year before my father died. I decided to slip it in here not to make weight, but because it's true as far as it goes. And because where it *doesn't* go interests me. Music, as Claude Debussy once pointed out, is the stuff between the notes.

What I didn't mention in the essay is that when my father escaped Czechoslovakia in 1948, he wasn't alone. Basically, I omitted my mother. In doing this—to keep from complicating the story, I told myself—I echoed Dad, who, two years earlier, had published his first book at the age of eighty-six, a full-length auto-biography called *Jdi po skryté stopě* (Go Down the Hidden Path) in which he managed almost entirely to leave out my mother. It was an act of revenge (for the years of belittling, for the "deflated balloon" comments) as elegant as it was cruel. All it required was the turn of one small grammatical lever—switching the first person from the plural to the singular—and she was erased. I survived, a slightly ghostly presence, more or less immaculately conceived.

I look at my father's book now, which sits on my shelf proudly autographed by the author, and I'm both appalled and thrilled by it. What could be more eloquent? What could express your feelings more clearly than to write the story of your life and leave out the person you'd shared it with for forty-six years? In one stroke he erased her, swept the table clean like Brando in *Streetcar*—"Now that's how I'm gonna clear the table." I didn't know the old man had it in him.

He sent her the book—neatly wrapped and signed. And my mother—she still had her mind, then—wrote back a week later to say how much she'd loved it. It was a grandmaster move on her part—swift and unanswerable. You could almost hear the pieces clicking the board, the hand slapping the timer—Queen takes Rook—checkmate.

A few days ago (I'm inserting this here because it's necessary— the other stories can wait) I went back to my father's book to pick up some "ballast"—my word for the facts and dates that keep the imagination on course—and found a reference to my mother. And then another. And a third. I read on, feeling slightly sick. How was this possible? How had I misremembered my father's book so completely? Had I *wanted* him to have left her out, to have gotten a little of his own back—and through him, a little of my own? What else had I imputed to him that wasn't true? I didn't go back to my writing that day. Or the next. I just reread my father's book, in Czech, cover to cover. It took me a week; at seven hundred pages, it's a big book. The more I read, the more *this* book, which I'd begun to think of as a kind of rescue operation, began to fade. All those facts and footnotes in my father's book. How could I ever compete with that apparatus, that knowing?

I seem to be one of those people doomed to rediscover things they've owned for decades—"Where did *this* come from? I *love* this jacket!" In this case it was the third-grade insight that you can be right and wrong at the same time. On the one hand, I'd been completely wrong: Though my mother's name *did* in fact fade out in the second half of the book, which devolved into a list of my father's academic awards and accomplishments, her name was everywhere in the first half: where she and my father had lived, how they'd escaped, who they'd known. In short, everything I'd said about my father exacting some kind of revenge on my mother by switching from the third person to the first was untrue—so wrong it felt malicious—a lie.

It wasn't a lie. Though her name was there, the human being was missing. What I'd remembered, typically, wasn't the fact but the spirit of the work, its essence. In my father's book my parents meet, they marry, they move here or there, but my mother's thoughts, her fears, her memories are absent. Not once does he imagine her inner world; not once does he enter her thoughts in any but the most banal way; though she moves and speaks and travels the world, she's all surface.

In truth, the literal erasure I'd imagined would have been far kinder. This was death by disinterest, something we've all glimpsed in certain marriages, hopefully not our own—that stage beyond fighting that signals the end of curiosity, that says, *I'm just not interested. We can remodel the kitchen and pay off the house, even fuck on schedule once a month, but I'll never ask you what you dream or fear, and if one night, driven by some desperation, you feel the need to tell me, I'll listen politely until you're done.*

It's a sin even Dante wouldn't touch.

And I'd lay it at my father's door if it were his, but I can't, because it wasn't. Oh, he tried all right, but the indifference was a sham, an act. To the end of his life—though he'd move on, remarry, pull himself out of the whirlpool of her descent—he never found the strength to stop caring about her, or to stop pretending he had. Here he was, standing in front of the door again, threatening to break it down, to trash the room and everything in it. This time he meant it. This time was for real. And having done it, he sent her the door. See? See what I've done?

And she saw right through him and thanked him for his efforts. Checkmate.

XXVII

I NOTICED HIM WHEN we walked into my father's memorial service in Prague—a slim man in his sixties, standing off to the side in the rain, smoking under an umbrella—and then the business of grief took over and I didn't see him again until we were leaving and he nodded at me with that slight tilt of the head that signals sympathy, regret, and he was gone.

It was only later that afternoon that my stepmother, herself numb with shock, asked if I'd noticed the slim man, maybe in his late sixties, standing by himself at the service. I had, I said. It was the strangest thing, she said—she hardly knew what to make of it. He'd said his name was Slouka, too, that he'd known my father, though not as well as he would have wished.

She was about to ask him who he was and how they'd met when a group of people interrupted to offer their condolences, and she lost track of him.

I never told her the tale my father had told me—I'm not sure why.

It's been two years. I haven't heard from my imagined uncle. I don't expect to.

XXVIII

"TIME ROBS US OF ALL, even of memory," Virgil reminds us in the *Eclogues*, his vision of a perfect, haunted world. Which is hardly news, not always the way it goes, and definitely not helpful. Still, even when it *is* the story, some memories hang on, linger like an afterimage in the mind's eye.

For my mother, the three crows she saw sitting on a branch just across the border dividing the Soviet and American sectors of Vienna while my father waited to be shot, would be one of the last to go. December, 1948. A cold, wet wind. The train didn't move. Two hundred meters away she could see the American MPs with their white helmets and white armbands. The two crows on the left, like rumpled old men, had sunk into their feathers; the third kept preening, digging under its wing with its beak. From a distance it seemed to be signaling.

She carried the image of those birds (for some reason I see them in the negative—three crow-shaped spaces on the outline of a branch) for more than sixty years. For all I know, she carries them still.

———

How we end up in a particular place at a particular time—say, waiting to be shot on a train in the Soviet sector of Vienna—is always due to a cast of characters and a sequence of events that have conspired to move us, block by block, to where we find ourselves. The trick to retrospection—assembling the cast, stringing together the events that explain the mess we're in—is designating a starting point, an original cause. It's an arbitrary business. Spin the wheel.

I'd nominate my father's father, Rheinhold Slouka, one of the three grandparents I never met, and the only one I would have wanted to. I have a few pictures of him—none as a younger man. In one, a family portrait taken in 1940 or so, he's standing to the left, formally dressed in dark suit and tie, his wife next to him, then my aunt Luba, maybe ten years old, and finally my father. I've spent a lot of time looking at that picture. There's something about his lean, almost English face, his kind, slightly burdened eyes, the quiet smile, that I like very much. He looks like a man used to keeping his own counsel, to making up his own mind, though whether these qualities are actually visible or just something I've imagined because of what I know, I can't say. What I *do* know is that Rheinhold Slouka seems to have been one of those human beings with an innate sense of their own worth, someone whose insistence on thinking for himself was only matched by his outrage toward those who'd question his right to do so.

He was also, apparently, born lucky—a reasonable thing to say about a man who survives his own hanging.

Though I told the story in a story called "Jumping Johnny," the "story" of Grandpa's execution happened to be true. During "the Great War," Rheinhold had served as a spy for the newly formed Czech legions operating with the Allies. It didn't go well.

It was my father who told me how my grandfather, at the age of twenty-two, had found himself marching south through warm rain to the Italian front, chosen for service in the espionage unit, sent over the lines, and, just like that, standing on a hardpack road with his arms tied behind his back watching a man he'd never met tie a noose on the end of a rope.

He knew exactly what was going to happen (by the time they came to him, after all, he'd watched forty or fifty of his comrades hoisted on the same horse, which was then simply walked toward the next tree until its burden slipped off its back), and yet, in spite of this, he went quietly, disbelieving, even as the rope was being slipped over his face, even as he felt the horse walking out from under him. The instant before his legs slid off the horse's back, before the sky and the leaves and the dark fringe of trees on the horizon began their mad, tilting dance, he noticed a bunch of cherries—tight-skinned and fat—on a low, dripping branch a meter from his face.

He jerked and thrashed like all the others—it must have made quite a sight, my father said, that three-kilometer alley of trees—except that after the others had stopped, he was still going. Seems they'd either left too much rope, or the branch had bent just enough, or the sides of the ditch in that particular place were just a bit narrower than elsewhere. When the Allied front came through later that afternoon, two men on horseback, one on either side of the lane, went from rope to rope with their bayonets, dropping the dead into the ditch. My grandfather was one of them.

Except he wasn't. Waking during the night, he crawled up on the road, cut the rope binding his wrists on a scythe he found leaning against a haystack, and started walking. Three weeks later, he was home. The only thing he had to show for it, said my father, who was born six years later, was a miniature tremble in his handwriting, as though his feet, leaving the back of that horse, had started a strange, nervous current, like death's own heartbeat. That was it, my father said. That and a photograph, the torn-off page of a magazine, in fact, that hung in the parlor throughout my father's childhood: inside its gray, handmade frame, below the white lettering of the magazine's name, *Domov a Svět*, it showed a wet country lane stretching to the horizon, cherry trees, and two converging lines of the dead. A journalist traveling with the front had taken the picture before the cavalry cut the men into the ditch. Browsing a stationery store less than a month after his return home, my grandfather recognized himself as the fourth man on the right.

He bought the magazine, neatly removed the cover, framed it, then hung the picture of his execution in the kitchen, where my father would sometimes find him, a bowl of cherries on the table next to him, studying it. Gloating. How many men, sentenced to hang by the neck until dead, lived to look at a photograph of themselves hanging by the neck? The experience cemented him in his disbelief, if any cement was needed, though it could just as easily have thrown him the other way.

What I'm getting at is that while my father inherited exactly nothing from his father in terms of money or property, in terms of what Nabokov called "un-real estate" his inheritance was considerable, including (along with a talent for storytelling and a streak of sentimentality), a hearty disrespect for organized religion, an extra measure of luck and a second helping of stubbornness. The third item would determine his behavior during the German occupation and after it; the second would allow him to survive the rain of crap it brought down on his head.

Which brings us to the next war. Just twenty years after a senseless squabble had left 15 million dead from Belgium to the Balkan Peninsula, the march of boots and the sound of 10,000 voices roaring in unison spread across Europe. Stamped out of the Austro-Hungarian Empire just twenty years earlier, its constitution proudly patterned on the Constitution of the United States, the tiny country of Czechoslovakia quickly found itself overwhelmed. Which didn't mean that there weren't some, like my father and grandfather (and others, infinitely braver), who didn't buck that tide instinctively, creatively, continually. There were quite a few.

Though the line between resistance and suicide could be hard to see in 1942, my father and grandfather seem to have walked it well. In retrospect, there was a certain, inherited "Daddy was a pistol, I'm a son-of-a-gun" thing going on: The abuse of power didn't sit well with either of them. At the same time, whatever mirroring there may have been was unconscious; neither spoke to the other about what he was doing, both denied they were doing anything at all. Whatever they accomplished, they accomplished separately, through a sort of unacknowledged and deadly form of parallel play I find hard to imagine: Small things mattered supremely—a single misstep could erase you.

My grandfather, appropriately, was better at the game: Older, more cautious, a family man operating under the terror of that responsibility, he understood that survival depended on keeping the circle small, blending in, doing your damage quietly. And Rheinhold, with his sleepy smile and his tall man's stoop, was a quiet one. When the betrayal at Munich in late 1938 made armed resistance impossible, the Czech legionnaires from the First World War had quickly gone underground, forming cells that would disrupt the German war effort at every opportunity; as a former legionnaire, Rheinhold was there from the beginning, keeping his mouth shut, doing his bit.

The keeping-his-mouth-shut part was key. Equally important was knowing when to play to expectation, to act the ignorant, subservient Slav. When in early 1939, for example, every household with a radio was issued an official, stick-on warning label (to be affixed to the radio's face) stating that listening to foreign broadcasts was a crime punishable by death, Rheinhold bowed his head, muttered *"Ich verstehe,"* and did as he was ordered: The sticker went on the family radio . . . its far right edge carefully aligned with the BBC's position on the dial. It saved all that time spent fiddling around, he said—truly, the Gestapo thought of everything.

With the exception of one terrifying week in 1942 during which the family secreted a Jewish man in the rabbit hutch behind the garden (I know neither the name of the man, nor whether he had anything to do with the assassination, that June, of Reichsprotektor Reinhard Heydrich, nor indeed, whether he even survived the war), the Sloukas' involvement in subversive activities was, to all appearances, nil. Which mattered; appearances were everything.

For well over three years, father and son kept each other in the dark, Rheinhold working with the legionnaires, my father with networks of young men primarily assigned the task of getting to the arms shipments dropped by parachute into the forests of Moravia before the Germans did, then rushing them through the woods on makeshift stretchers made from tree branches and coats to the barns and stables of sympathizers. Unbelievably, they managed it—each convinced the other was going about his day—until early 1944.

That winter, to aid the disastrous German retreat from Leningrad, the Occupation Authority requisitioned all the cross-country skis in the Protectorate, one of those slightly surreal details whose very simplicity carries the ring of truth. Russian winters came with snow. Snow was hard to walk in. Ten thousand frostbitten troops could use all the help they could get. What better way to acquire thousands of pairs of cross-country skis instantly than to take them from those who already had them?

The Czechs, inspired by the Gestapo's customary "under penalty of death" incentive program, hurried to comply; spiky mountains of cross-country skis piled up at the collection depots, not a few of them modestly decorated with tiny, black beauty spots along a fifteen-centimeter section just behind the upturn of the ski; handpainted along the rail, inconspicuous and symmetrical, the dots hid small-diameter holes drilled through the part of the ski certain to receive the greatest pressure when in use. Shipped en masse to the front, they'd hold up for a kilometer, then snap with a sound like a gunshot: Life was full of small pleasures.

On the day in question in 1944, my father and his friend, Mirek Vlach, were in the toolshed busily doctoring a ski when my father happened to look up to find *his* father, who was supposed to be at work, leaning in the doorway in his shirtsleeves. He had no idea how long he'd been standing there. There was nothing for my father to say: For two years he'd been righteously assuring his father that he'd taken his orders to heart, that—like him—he was keeping himself out of it, being smart.

My father waited by the vise, unsure of where this would go. His father lost his temper rarely—when he did, you wanted to be somewhere else. He glanced at Mirek, whose face seemed stuck in a permanent wince.

"How long?" my grandfather said.

"Not long," my father said.

My grandfather didn't say anything.

"Two years," my father said.

Nothing.

"Three."

My grandfather looked at him for a while, then nodded toward the vise: "Don't get greedy," he said. "Six are enough, one-point-five centimeters apart. And watch out for Čermák—he can see the door from his window." And he left.

Fifteen months later, the war was over. I don't know if they celebrated together, but I like to think they did: father and son, the celebratory clink of the shot glasses of *slivovice*, then back to work.

XXIX

BACK IN THE 1970S, walking through the small, cobbled towns of Moravia, I'd often find myself waved over by people working in their yards—hoeing a garden, say, or building a wall—who'd somehow spotted my Western-style jeans or sneakers. They'd ask where I was from, then offer me a glass of home-made wine, or dinner, or a place to sleep, eager to show their hospitality to someone from the West. Our conversations would take place in freezing little wine cellars dug deep into the ground (heavy coats would always be hanging on pegs outside the entrance), or in tiny dining rooms with plastic tablecloths where, sooner or later, I'd be shown the hidden bust of Tomas Masaryk—the Czechs' George Washington and, since 1948, a forbidden symbol of national independence.

I remember those people still, though the years have blurred their particular features into qualities: pouched eyes and moles and laborers' hands, into generosity, curiosity, pride. We talked about many things over the course of those afternoons and evenings, but one thing I remember hearing over and again, which troubled and confused me, was that in some ways the war had been preferable to what had followed it. In 1942, the consensus was, you generally knew who your enemy was: He wore a uniform. He spoke German. He could be shot. After the Communist coup in 1948, the lines blurred; the enemy was your professor, your neighbor, your brother-in-law. The rot was inside now. If summary executions and mass deportations were no longer the order of the day, lives were being destroyed nonetheless, decade after decade, with no end in sight. There was more. In 1942 or '43 there'd at least been victories to hope for—now there was nothing. The West had no business here, the Berlin wall was the wall, and those who refused to join the Party were out of luck. Reduced to their sense of humor and their appreciation for the absurd, they watched the years pass.

Twenty years later, fifteen years after the Velvet Revolution had consigned both the German and Soviet occupations to history, I asked my father if the opinions I'd heard back in the seventies— that the postwar years were worse than the war itself—surprised him. We were sitting at a "café" inside a horrible little mall on Vinohradská Street surrounded by mostly deserted, expensive stores—Montblanc, Versace, Louis Vuitton—catering to bulked-out Russian men and pneumatic women in leopard-print bustiers. Above us, hanging from the interior balcony in front of the second-floor stores, enormous posters of gorgeous models looked down on the Czechs who couldn't afford their sunglasses.

My father, in his old-man's beret, had hung his cane on the fake café "railing." People were people—it was natural to see today's enemy as worse than yesterday's; still, he suspected the Jews might have a different take. And then there was the fact that Czechoslovakia had suffered considerably less during the war than Poland, for example; nostalgia for the Reich might be a tougher sell in Warsaw. He shrugged, took a sip of his vodka: Anyway, the Nazis for six years or the Soviets for forty—these were the options?

Remembering this some twelve years later still, a garish February sunset reddening the frozen hills outside my window and the mercury dropping like a stone, I realize it was precisely this unwillingness to sacrifice complexity to convenience (or convention), this refusal to choose door number one over door number two out of laziness or exhaustion or the desire to please anyone-the-fuck-at-all, even himself, that I loved most about my father, that I miss the most now that he's gone, and that probably marked his life most profoundly. It makes sense that it would have. By 1948, throughout the Eastern Bloc, the Lie was just getting its legs; ideological conformity was the order of the day. In that climate, men (and women) of my father's stripe were uniquely unsuited for survival.

The facts spoke for themselves, after all: He'd survived the Germans for six years; after the Communist coup, he barely lasted six months.

XXX

ACTION AND REACTION: WHERE Big History is concerned, some sequence is believable—thing follows thing. And so, a brief recap: In 1938, betrayed at Munich (not only will England and France not come to their aid, the Czechs are told, but should they choose to defend themselves, the decision will be construed by their former allies as an act of war), Czechoslovakia is thrown to Germany—a steak to keep the dog at bay. It's a bad move—the steak just makes the dog stronger, hungrier: The country's munitions and its considerable industrial might are promptly absorbed by the Reich, then turned against the appeasers. A few months later, Germany invades Poland. England, at long last seeing the light, declares war. Six years and approximately 50 million lives later, the Axis powers are defeated and the Reich stopped, 988 years short of its 1,000-year goal. Soviet armies, albeit with some excesses (forcing young girls to be hidden in coal piles), liberate Czechoslovakia.

Thing follows thing: In 1945, the war finally over, 2.9 million ethnic Germans are summarily booted out of Czechoslovakia, sometimes brutally, often extralegally, still more often unjustly, and, at least on some visceral level, understandably. Thanks to the horse trading at Yalta, Czechoslovakia is now under the Soviet sphere of influence. Initially at least—one of history's little ironies—a significant number of Czechs are just fine with this. Grateful to the Russians for their liberation, with the West's betrayal at Munich still fresh in their minds, they're not indisposed: Papa Stalin's off in Moscow, a long way away. As for the Communist Party of Czechoslovakia, well, compared to its equivalents in Yugoslavia or Poland (where members of the wartime Resistance are being arrested and pogroms are accomplishing what pogroms are meant to accomplish), the KSC is a shining light, a responsible party in the ruling coalition.

From here, things proceed quickly, and—at least in retrospect—predictably. Initially inclined to participate in the Marshall Plan, the Czech government is forced to back out by the Kremlin, which suddenly feels a whole lot closer. In 1947, the Czech prime minister and Communist Party leader Klement Gottwald is summoned by Papa to Moscow, spanked, and told to get cracking; on his return home, Gottwald demands more power for the Communist Party, then forces President Beneš's hand. Beneš holds out for a while, and then, fearing Soviet military intervention, capitulates. The date is February 25, 1948. By this point, the writing is on the wall; nothing it says is ambiguous.

Still, some maintain, not all the lights have gone out. Though the Communist Party has consolidated power, though the Soviet Union—having used the three years since the end of the war to recover and strengthen its position—has begun to assert itself, a few holdouts, most notably the Czech foreign minister and son of the first president, Jan Masaryk, are still standing—candles against the dark and so forth. Until March 10, 1948, that is, when Jan Masaryk commits suicide by flying out of his window (leaving scratch marks on the wallpaper and feces smeared on the floor) and the lights, most definitely, go out.

Throughout all this, my father, like some wannabe Edward R. Murrow, continues to wave the banner of the fourth estate. Genetically programmed to stubbornness (as well as probably wanting to impress his older, more experienced colleagues), he misses the fact that windows generally outnumber journalists. What's happening in Czechoslovakia—the lies, the propaganda, the purges—is an outrage; the press alone can, no, *must* continue to report the truth. Which is an admirable position, a just position, a position reminiscent of a certain Stephen Crane poem: "Have you ever made a just man?" / "Oh, I've made three," answered God / "But two of them are dead, / And the third— / Listen! Listen! / And you will hear the thud of his defeat." Just so.

Meanwhile, because people will fall in love in bomb shelters as well as on tropical beaches, my mother and F. continue to stand before the door to the Law, waiting for something to happen. To what extent they're aware of what's happening around them and to what extent they inhabit a country all their own—as people in love often do—is hard to say. My guess, since neither is stupid and F.'s patriotic bona fides as a former Green Beret are beyond question, is that like most people caught in great historical moments they see the unfolding situation in alternating flashes of clarity and confusion: aware of the danger but unsure of its depth, aware that something must change but unsure of what, wanting to be together yet realizing, dimly, that the city of Brno, like the country around it, like the continent of Europe, has begun to move under their feet.

XXXI

SOMETHING HAD TO CHANGE. It did.

In March, 1948, not long after Jan Masaryk's "suicide" ("A very tidy man," the Czech joke went, "so tidy that when he committed suicide by jumping out the window, he remembered to close it behind him"), a man in his early fifties with a vaguely intellectual air—the pipe, the coat, the quietly observant attitude—approached my twenty-three-year-old father on his way home from work. They wouldn't speak long.

Names weren't important, he said, declining to shake my father's hand in public. He'd come straight to the point: Rheinhold Slouka was a legionnaire. His son, aside from being an idealistic fool—but let it go—was Rheinhold's son. It was for the sake of a fellow legionnaire, and for *only* that reason, that he was sticking his neck out and passing on this bit of news: Lists were being drawn up. My father's name was on one of them. He had a week, maybe less, to make whatever arrangements necessary to escape the country. Personally, he'd go with "less." Rheinhold, of course, knew nothing about this, nor should he. And the man told my father the name and address of a *pašerák*, a smuggler—no, of course he couldn't write it down—and left.

In many ways, it was like preparing for any trip: You needed documents. You had to pack. You had to figure out how to get to where you were going, how much it would cost, who would take you. Finally, and this was fairly important, you had to decide how many were in your party.

Which is where the narrative of my parents' lives, like the path in Frost's yellow wood, splits in two: To the end of his days my father would maintain that he came to my mother the same evening he was told that he had to leave the country. They both knew that their marriage was in trouble, he said to her—it wasn't hard to see. He wouldn't ask her to come with him. He would get across if he could, set himself up, then send word. If she chose to join him, they'd try to make a go of it in exile; if not, he'd understand.

My mother's version of events, told with the same conviction, repeated through the decades, was the exact opposite. Coming home that evening, my father told her he'd been warned he had to escape Czechoslovakia before he was arrested. He was leaving it in her hands: If she came with him, they'd make a go of it together; if she chose to stay, he'd stay as well and hope for the best. It amounted to blackmail: If she stayed and my father was arrested, as he most likely would be, his imprisonment (or execution) would be on her conscience. She didn't want to go, my mother said, didn't want to leave her country, didn't believe it would be over nearly as soon as everyone said it would. She had no choice.

"I shall be telling this with a sigh / somewhere ages and ages hence / two [stories] diverged in a yellow wood . . ." In some ways it's almost beautiful, this twice-told tale—so perfectly calibrated, so delicately balanced a single grain of fact could move it. I'll never have that grain, that breath that causes one pan or the other to dip—with both of them gone, it's frozen for good.

I don't mind, really, and the fact that I don't, that I can live with these irreconcilable opposites, makes me wonder whether the competing stories I was told as a kid—one truth from column A, another from column B—played some small part in shaping me into who I am. What better way to make a writer—or a schizophrenic, I suppose—than to have a single child, isolate him, provide a steady diet of opposing and irreconcilable versions of "the facts," and wait?

One way or the other—and my guess is that the "truth" lies somewhere between the two stories, that my parents' decision was complicated from the get-go by hope, jealousy, guilt, fear (as well as the excitement of taking the plunge), then obscured under strata of self-justifying hindsight, remorse, resentment—they left together. My father, believing the warning he'd been given, made arrangements with the *pašerák*.

As exotic as it sounds, arranging to be smuggled out of your own country was in many ways a practical, even mundane transaction: somebody had to get you from point A to point B; you worked out the details—price, meeting place, time, etc.—more or less the way you'd set up a ride to the airport. Except this wasn't a ride to the airport. For one thing, the men capable of getting you there—those likely to know the terrain, the fences, the timing of guard patrols, etc.—weren't always the gentlest souls. For another, refugees were easy prey. They carried everything of value they owned. Nobody knew they were going. More to the point—as the bodies with the gold fillings torn from their mouths along the Austrian border testified—nobody would know if they didn't arrive.

I don't know what my mother's thoughts were during those last few days—whether she spoke to F., whether he knew she was leaving. Whether he tried to dissuade her if he did. All I know is that, for whatever reasons, she went with my father, and that when she did, something inside her froze.

And so one afternoon in March, 1948, my mother and father got on the train in Brno with a suitcase each. It was a day of wet snow. Their destination was a small town near the Austrian border. They were to report to a certain address. They would wait there until 1 a.m., at which time the *pašerák* would take them through the forests to the place where, earlier that night, he'd cut a hole in the fences, at the time still free of current. The guards were on a twelve-minute schedule.

Bits and pieces of that night would remain vivid to them for the rest of their lives, a shared memory no amount of time or animosity could erase: the weight of their suitcases, the cold smell of the pines, the slipperiness of the wet snow on the trail. Reading the path by the openings in the trees over their heads, the *pašerák*—a gruff man with grotesquely outsized hands—moved quickly; my father, to keep from losing him, kept his left hand on his shoulder, my mother, in turn, kept her hand on my father's.

Crouched in the dark, watching the wavering beam of the guards' light pass below them, they waited till the smuggler rose, then followed him quickly to the place where he'd cut the fence. The hole had been repaired.

The situation was immediately clear to them all: The border guards were alerted to a possible escape attempt. The schedule meant nothing. Quite possibly, they were dead already—a rifle might flare in the dark at any moment. Which left only one question: Retreat or continue? They made the decision instantly: Push on, use the available minutes. Lifting my father on his shoulders the way a father lifts a child so it can dive into the water, the smuggler brought him almost to the level of the top wire. My father threw himself over into the snowy mud, rolled, recovered. My mother came next, handed over the top strand like a parcel of goods, followed by the suitcases. And the *pašerák* was gone.

My parents made it to the woods, vanished. Four hours later, slogging across snow-covered fields thawing into mud, they arrived at a rural train station outside Vienna. It was just after dawn. The goal was to make it from the Russian sector—Vienna at the time was cut like a pie into Soviet, French, British, and American slices—to the American, and from there to the French.

If the goal was simple, realizing it wouldn't be. The issue, the one issue above all others, involved the stolen papers they'd bought—my father's in particular: Under the pressure of time, drawing on the tiny, time-sensitive supply of citizenship papers stolen daily from Austrian citizens or "borrowed" from the recently dead before the authorities could circulate their names, the fence had been unable to find a good visual match for my father: Kurt Habermann looked nothing like him. The fence apologized, offered my father his money back; if he'd had another week, maybe two . . .

A decent man, he told them the truth. My mother, he said, would most likely get through. The papers were under different names—they'd have to remember to take off their wedding rings—and would ideally allow them to travel from the Westbahnhof station to Ennsbrucke. My father's odds, he regretted to say, were not good. Worse, actually. His Czech accent was not the problem—the Russian guards spoke barely a word of German and were either too nationalistic or too stupid to employ native speakers to ferret out the escapees—the problem was the picture itself. My father might get lucky, of course, and if the issue came down to certain arrest at home versus possible arrest on the border there was no choice . . . still, it was a shame. If only he'd had more time.

He had a final word of advice: A few days earlier, the husband of a couple trying to escape together had been caught and ordered off the train. Realizing that his life was done (within two or three minutes he'd be executed behind the station), unable to acknowledge his wife with so much as a glance, much less say goodbye or kiss her, the man had taken their one suitcase off the rack like a sleepwalker and stumbled off the train. His wife, in shock, continued on, not only a widow, but a penniless one. His advice, if it came to it—and he sincerely hoped it wouldn't—was simple enough: Leave the luggage.

The astonishing thing is that they made it as far as they did. Needing to blend in with the early morning commuters going in to the city, my mother and father had done what they could. Before

My dad and his family, around the beginning of the war. He's on the right.
Rheinhold, my grandfather, is on the left.

Dad

Mom during the war, maybe seventeen years old.

Mom outside her childhood home. Her mother looks on in a polka-dot dress.

27433

DEUTSCHES REICH — NĚMECKÁ ŘÍŠE.
PROTEKTORAT BÖHMEN UND MÄHREN — PROTEKTORÁT ČECHY A MORAVA.

Zahl
Čís. 80 80

HEIMATSCHEIN · DOMOVSKÝ LIST

Olga K U B Í K   Olga K U B Í K O V Á

Studentin   studentka
Beruf oder Beschäftigung   povolání nebo zaměstnání
19.II.1925   19.II.1925
Geburtsdaten   data narození
ledig   svobodná
Stand   stav

hat in Brünn das Heimatsrecht seit   má v Brně právo domovské od

Geburt, der Vater seit 1903.   narození, otec od 1903.

Brünn, am   28.V.1942.   19
V Brně dne

Der Regierungskommissar: — Vládní komisař.

_____

Eigenhändige Unterschrift der Partei.
Vlastnoruční podpis osoby, které se domovský list vydává

Streng verrechenbare Drucksorte Nr. 5
R. M. Rohrer, Brünn. — 1610-42

The German Reich's document giving my seventeen-year-old mother
permission to live in her own country.

F. as a young man.

My mom teaching
English at the language
camp where she met F.,
summer 1946.

F.—the famous skiing photo.

Mom and dad with a
friend, somewhere in
Germany, early 1950s.

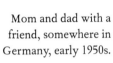

Mom and dad with a
friend, Sydney, 1951.

Mom in some unidentified
train station, circa 1948.

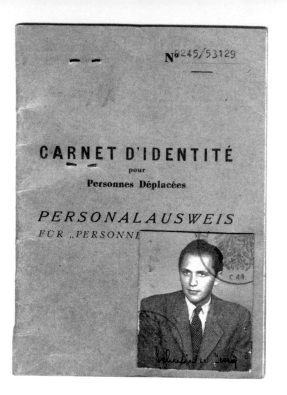

The document identifying my mom and dad as official refugees.

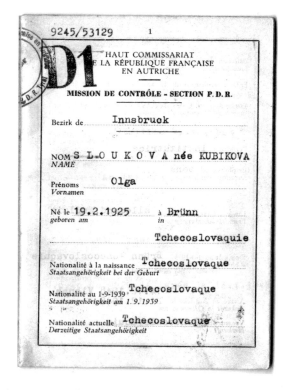

9245/53129   1

D1

HAUT COMMISSARIAT
DE LA RÉPUBLIQUE FRANÇAISE
EN AUTRICHE

MISSION DE CONTRÔLE - SECTION P. D. R.

Bezirk de   **Innsbruck**

NOM   **S L O U K O V A née KUBIKOVA**
NAME

Prénoms   **Olga**
Vornamen

Né le **19.2.1925**   à **Brünn**
geboren am   in

       Tchecoslovaquie

Nationalité à la naissance **Tchecoslovaque**
Staatsangehörigkeit bei der Geburt

Nationalité au 1-9-1939 **Tchecoslovaque**
Staatsangehörigkeit am 1.9.1939

Nationalité actuelle **Tchecoslovaque**
Derzeitige Staatsangehörigkeit

The good times in Australia. Mom and dad are on the far right.
The others are Czech refugees/friends. Circa 1950.

Mom arriving in the New World, the Statue of Liberty in the background.

Dad, New York skyline.

Mom and Dad, probably at Lost Lake, in the early years in America.

Mom and me, Jones Beach, New York.

Forest Hills, New York,
circa 1960.

Me using dad as a jungle gym.

Archery lesson, summer morning, Lost Lake.

Me and mom, around 1974.

Mom with Uncle Pepa and Sonya.

My mother and her father, František Kubík, 1970s.

Me, mom, and our friends, 1976. Jiřinka is in the second row, far left. Mirek Vlach, with whom my father was in the underground as a teenager, is in the back row, far left.

My mom with her friends after she returned home to Czechoslovakia.
Jiřinka is in the window.

Mom and F., reunited. She always said it was a bad picture of him, and it was.

Mom in Bethlehem, Pennsylvania, the ghosts piling on.

Mom on Palm Beach, Australia. One of my favorite pictures of her.

arriving at the station they'd cleaned the mud off their clothes, wiping off the worst with handfuls of snow. My mother put on a bit of lipstick; my father adjusted his tie. They stood out like giraffes on a roof. Waiting on the train platform, their suitcases smeared with mud, their shoes squelching water, they might as well have been carrying a sign: CZECH REFUGEES—SHOOT US.

For whatever reason, maybe because they *were* so obvious, or so young, nobody said a thing; now and then a man or woman would look at them while chatting to a friend or over the top of a newspaper, then look away. The train came. They got on it. Now, at least, they could take off their coats without drawing attention. Not talking or looking at each other, as they hadn't since coming out of the woods, they took their seats.

And then, before the platform outside had even screeched to a halt, a guard in a Soviet Army uniform, no more than seventeen or eighteen years old, had jumped on board and was making his way up the car. Holding a cigarette, he'd wave his fingers for the documents, check the offered papers and toss them back. Sometimes he'd take a long drag while looking at the papers' owner, release a blue wall of smoke up past his mustache, and only then hand them back. Once or twice—unsmiling, aware of being the center of attention—he'd call something to his comrade, working his way toward him from the back.

Careful not to appear nervous by seeming too relaxed, my father glanced out the window, then across the aisle at the people opposite, then tilted his head slightly and pressed his thumb into his cheek as if testing a toothache. The kid was six rows ahead; the arm with the cigarette abruptly rose in a half-salute, then dropped to his side. Five rows ahead. Four. The terror was a distant voice trying to get your attention, like pain under anesthesia.

And then he was there and my father had reached into the vest pocket of his jacket for his papers and the kid had glanced at them, said something to his friend and handed them back. Irritable now, increasingly impatient, he took my mother's papers, paused to look her up and down, lingering offensively, and handed them back. A minute later, finished with the car, the two made their way to the front where the other guard pushed open the door and stepped off the train. Someone out on the platform laughed.

And just like that, it was over. They were through. Somehow, unbelievably, it was over. In ten minutes they'd be handing their papers to the American MPs. It was over. My mother could smell the winter smell of the car. It smelled of melting snow and leather.

At the front of the car the kid with the mustache turned, looked down the aisles. Moving his head slightly as his eyes ticked from face to face, he went carefully, row by row—when he came to my mother he had it. *Vy!* he called, pointing at my father. You! The sweat leaped out on my father's forehead as instantly as if he'd been lowered into an oven. He glanced to his left and right, then back to the guard—*Ich?* The kid yelled something in Russian, then switched to German: *Du—auf!* You, out.

From somewhere outside, someone yelled something in Russian and the kid jerked his head slightly as if to look out. My father started to get up, began gathering his coat. *Du! Auf! Schnell!* Again someone yelled something from outside: My mother recognized the Russian word for "girls," worked it out from there—"Fool— we've got girls here."

My father picked up his hat, dropped it, picked it up again, folded his coat over his arm.

Again the voice from outside: "Get out here, you asshole—what're you doing?"

My father began walking toward the front of the car. He fumbled his coat, dropped it.

"Get out here, you idiot!"

Again the kid glanced outside, then back at my father, still making his snail's progress up the aisle, then slapped the air with disgust and rushed off the train. My father stopped, unsure of what to do, then made his way back to his seat and sat down. He didn't look at my mother.

And nothing happened. Nobody looked at them. The train didn't move. Now and then there were voices from outside. The brakes hissed. A hundred meters away, three crows sat on the bare branch of a tree behind the American line—one of them, preening, seemed to be signaling something. They'd been there forever. They would always be there.

My father aged over those few minutes, my mother said. He didn't move, he didn't speak—it seemed he didn't breathe. He didn't look at her. He just sat there, watching the open door at the front of the car, almost calm except for the sweat streaming down his face, which he couldn't help, the muscles in his face flinching each time the brakes hissed, each time the train lurched, then settled, each time a voice yelled something in Russian from the platform. And then the brakes released again and the train lurched back, then forward and began to move, the platform crawling by almost imperceptibly, so slowly anyone could still step on board, then faster, so that a man would have to jog, then faster—and time resumed its flow. Minutes later my parents were in the American zone and not long after, the French, where their documents were examined with a typically Gallic mixture of weariness and amusement and they were officially recognized as refugees. They carried two mud-smeared suitcases. In most ways that matter they'd remain refugees for forty years.

I like to think about the girl on the platform—the one who looked so fine in her sweater, her heels, who saved my father from a bullet to the brain, who inadvertently extended his life another sixty-four years, allowing me to be born, to marry a certain girl from Florida, allowing the two of us to have the (grown) children we have. . . . I'd like to find her—an old woman in her late eighties now, living in Vienna a block or two from a small *beserlpark*, where she still likes to walk when the weather's good. I'd like to thank her.

With one long-fingered hand on her hip, the other pulling back her hair to accept a light, she let my parents go, allowed them to carry their burden of memories and dreams a little further down the road. Can't ask for more than that.

XXXII

AT THE BOTTOM OF Wenceslas Square in Prague one summer
evening years ago, maneuvering through the crowd of Russian
mafiosos in leather jackets and Czech dads with their little girls
sitting on their shoulders, hands locked like seat belts around
their fathers' foreheads, past the German and Italian tourists and
the hookers and the shirtless Brit vomiting into the tulips on the
central island . . . there, amid various Bad Art installations I came
across a human skeleton sitting on a box. He was seated inside
a crude wooden cage, like an orangutan at the zoo. I stopped.
Around us the crowd babbled multilingually—a beautiful evening. He was leaning forward, elbows on his kneecaps, bony
hands turned out at the wrists. His attitude was both querulous
and resigned, aggressive and beseeching. "What?" he seemed to
be saying. "Tell me what the fuck you want?"

I want truth. And while I'm at it, justice for all.

I'll settle for what I can get.

———

Two days ago, I received a note from the director of the care home my mother's been "living" in for the past year or so. A compassionate soul, she wanted to warn me: I had to prepare myself.

I wrote back to thank her, because she was kind and because I was grateful. I didn't tell her that the person I'd loved had been gone for years; that when it came to my mother it was complicated—a stew of love and outrage, recrimination and regret—complicated. That when it came to my mother, things didn't follow from A to Z, love didn't rise or decline like the stock market, revelations didn't appear on schedule.

In the fall of 1991, after my parents had separated, my father suffered a massive heart attack. I flew to Bethlehem, slept in the waiting room of the IC unit. My wife, pregnant with our daughter, arrived with our two-year-old son a few days later. The next day, Mom flew in from Prague. And the madness commenced. She staggered around the halls of the hospital, weeping, yelling at me, at my father in his coma, at the staff—who finally threatened to have her removed—claiming we were all conspiring against her. She got the keys to my father's apartment from the hospital closet and went through his letters, then read them aloud to me, raging over the beeping of the monitors. She refused to pick up our son, claiming we thought she was filthy.

It was sometime during those insane days, which I thought might end with the two of us strangling each other over my father's body, that an old friend of my parents, who'd come to offer his support, took me aside in the hallway. He'd appeared three after-noons in a row, bringing food, staying out of the way.

He'd been in psychiatric practice for forty-five years, he said, but he was speaking to me now as a friend, not a doctor. He needed me to hear him.

"She will destroy you," he said, putting his hand on my shoul-der, and then he said it again. "You have a young family, what seems like a good marriage . . . I know what I'm talking about. You have to distance yourself. You won't save her."

I was so taken aback that I didn't thank him. I'm doing it now.

I'd needed to hear what I'd known in my heart for a long time. It didn't mean I could act on it.

Fifteen years earlier, the winter of my freshman year of college, I had a dream which I wrote down in my journal so I could forget it. In the dream my mother and I were on a boat in the middle of a blue ocean tacked tight to the horizon. Everything was still: the boat, its reflection, the pale hot circle of the sun.

My mother decided to go for a swim. Far off, she was calling for help, her arms flailing in the air. I was there instantly. Crazy with fear, she grabbed onto my shoulders and neck as if I were a board flung into the water. I tried to drag her back to the boat, but I couldn't do it—her terror had given her outrageous strength. She fought and twisted as though shot through by some giant current. Holding her across her chest and under her arm, as I'd learned to do in lifesaving class, choking and strangling, I somehow dragged her to the surface, only to be pulled under again and again.

It was then that I realized she was swimming down. I could feel her pulling into the dark, reaching for my face, my throat, and I began to fight, striking down with my fists, desperate to separate myself from this thing which only moments before I'd been determined to save, and woke myself with such a spasmodic wrench of my body that I knocked my glasses off the reading table by my dormitory bed.

XXXIII

OVER THE SEASONS, AS I've worked on these pages, I've kept a particular photograph of my mother on my desk. Hardly bigger than a postage stamp, it's become a kind of talisman; wherever I write—in motel rooms, in the Reading Room at the New York Public Library—I have it on the table next to me. It was taken on January 1, 1952, at Palm Beach in Sydney, Australia. I know this because my mother wrote the place and date, in blue ink, on the back.

Of all the pictures I have of her, and I have many, this may be my favorite. The cloudy, southern hemisphere sky is marred by two small water spots, the cottony surf blurs in the foreground. My mother, not quite twenty-seven years old, is coming out on the beach. She's holding what looks like a bathing cap filled with water, intended for the person taking the picture—almost certainly my father.

It's hard to analyze why we love what we do, but here goes nothing.

I love this picture because the joy it captures seems so big, so sovereign, it should have been able to hold its own against anything that came afterward. I love it because it couldn't. I love it because as a kid I heard the echoes of that joy—hours of contentment and laughter and who-knows-what that have come to feel slightly unreal to me, and for that reason all-the-more precious. I love it, finally, because it seems to support what I want to believe I remember: that my mother was able to keep the demons out for months and even years at a time before they finally forced the lock.

But what do I know, really?—what's visible is always dwarfed by what's not. I can tell you that my mother's happy in that photograph even though F's not there, even though it's been four years since she's seen him, two years or more since she's had a letter from him, and that this is significant somehow, but for all I know she's full of joy because just seconds before the shutter froze her, she recalled splashing him by the side of some reedy pond and the memory of his body came over her like a wave and suddenly giddy with groundless hope, she scooped a capful of water from the surf.

I'll never know. I can study her face with the magnifying glass, but she's hidden away from me. Which is as it should be. When they invent the technology that can unlock her laughter, I'll know I've lived too long.

XXXIV

I HAVE THE DOCUMENTS from the years that followed: the foreign-worker cards and the soft, well-worn passports with their photos and their purple stamps, the information (hair: brown; face: oval) filled in with a fountain pen. I have pictures of them—in Innsbruck, in Sydney, in Munich and New York—and the fact that they're so young fills me with wonder and something like jealousy: How much they'd lived by the time they were thirty.

Taken together, the letters and the telegrams and the Carnets d'Identité pour Personnes Deplacées tell a familiar story, a story not that different from that of the Syrian or Sudanese refugees in today's paper: a tale of dislocation and loss, of men and women and children officially "displaced," drifting from port to port before eventually landing, through a combination of perseverance and ingenuity and maybe even luck (though only time can answer that), in the West. It's an important story, but it's not the real story where my parents are concerned, and if I told it straight and safe, following the trail of bread crumbs, I'd be leaving out everything essential. Facts are just scaffolding for the heart.

That said, in my parents' case the scaffolding was interesting enough. For a year and a half, before they could get berths on a ship for Australia—the only country besides Brazil that would accept immigrant couples, not just men—they survived in the refugee camps outside Innsbruck. It was a hard time made bearable by youth, by the company of others (as in "misery loves . . .") and, eventually, by the softening passage of time: At the time, the winter was long, fuel scarce, food communally scrounged.

What remains of our lives, of the hours of plotting and hope, of the taste of a particular meal—never mind the river of impressions and dreams that runs under our conscious day? Not much—a handful of names, misremembered dates, a few anecdotes retold much too often. Live long enough, the past caramelizes into fiction.

Still, maybe because it left a space, one story from their days in Innsbruck seemed to matter to them, and for that reason to me. It can stand in for the many.

Though the giddiness of making it across the border carried them a while—for the rest of his life my father would maintain that the bratwurst he bought on the platform in Innsbruck as the wind chilled the sweat on his back was the best thing he ever ate—it didn't take long for reality to take off its shoe and pound it on the table. They were nothing now. Whatever rights they'd had, or could at least lay claim to, were gone. For the next three years, like leaves in a spring flood, they'd go where the tide of *personnes deplacées* would take them, herded into camps, formed into lines, escorted by immigration authorities and Italian *carabinieri* from trucks to trains to ships, from holding station to holding station, meal to meal. From now on, whatever privileges might be bestowed on them, from the right to travel to the right to work, whatever aid they might receive—a slice of bread, a bed to sleep in—would be at the discretion of whatever nation allowed them inside its borders.

Like soldiers nostalgic for the camaraderie of battle, they would look back on those years as a time of friendship, friendship fueled by mutual poverty, by small victories—a kilo of lemons, a purple stamp on a visa—made large by circumstance. It wasn't just the obvious truth—that within certain limits, having less means living more; it wasn't just the romance of youth. It was about distraction. In my mother's case, survival distracted her from herself, suppressed her capacity for giving herself pain. Ironically—or maybe entirely predictably—it would be the New World, with its wall-to-wall carpeting and its fifty-seven flavors, that would defeat her. No longer required to fight, sitting in her bedroom switching from *Days of Our Lives* to *The Edge of Night*, she'd begin to devour herself.

But here I am, the morbid son, flying on ahead, bringing bad news. In the winter of 1948–49, my parents' future lay in embryo. They were living on the nick of time. They had two suitcases. They had their lives. It was enough.

Which is not to say, "easy." In the refugee camps around Innsbruck in the winter of 1948, there was no work and little food. A black market existed, but the risks were considerable. Securing passage to one of the countries accepting refugees could take years. Complicating things even more was the usual congregation of criminals that appears, attracted by some frequency of desperation, wherever refugee communities form—many of them refugees themselves. My parents had to be careful, keep their distance, avoid getting drawn in at all costs.

One name in particular seemed to float to the surface of every conversation. Vikin was no joke, people said. A sociopath with the deceptive good looks and lank brown hair of an American movie star, he'd stabbed a man through the throat in Jindřichův Hradec, then escaped across the border a step ahead of the law. A thief, a smuggler, a card sharp known to the authorities in Budapest and Prague, he was ferociously quick with a knife, utterly mercurial. He'd made a space for himself around Innsbruck, coming and going as he pleased, doing what he wanted; even other criminals stayed out of his way.

Though I have few particulars, less than a week passed before my father, standing at a tram stop, let's say, was asked if he had the time, in German, by a man in a long coat. My father hitched up his sleeve to look at his watch—the last thing of any value in his possession. It was just after three, he answered. The man grinned, placing the accent. "You're Czech," he said, switching over from German.

He was, my father said.

"Where from?"

"Brno," my father said.

"You're kidding—you're from Brno?" the man said. "Do you know Tonda Pazourek?"

Of course, my father said. He'd known Pazourek since he was a kid. They'd been on the same track team at the Gymnasium—lousy runner, stand-up guy.

The tram came. They got on and kept talking. My father liked him. Coming to his stop, he introduced himself. "Zdenek Slouka," he said, extending his hand. "I'd buy you a drink if I could afford it."

"Vikin," the man said, and smiled: "We'll see what we can do about that."

Vikin, it turned out, could do a great deal, beginning with the bottle he brought to their room the next day.

How had he found them? my parents asked.

It wasn't difficult, he said—a young couple, just arrived from Brno . . . He smiled. If he'd known how beautiful the wife was—he said this so gently, almost regretfully, that my mother couldn't help but smile—it would have been even easier.

It was my beautiful mother who tackled it head-on. They'd heard some things, she said.

Things?

About him.

He wasn't surprised, he said.

Were they true?

Such as . . . ?

Was he a card sharp?

He knew his way around a deck, yes.

She told him about the man in Jindřichův Hradec.

He hadn't heard that one yet, he said.

Was it true?

He looked at her for a long second. "The last time I was in Jindřichův Hradec, I was ten. I don't remember stabbing anyone." He paused. "It would be nice if you could keep that to yourself— we don't want to confuse people."

To say that Vikin got my parents through those eighteen months would be overstating it a bit; to say he was their friend would not. A month after their arrival, with my parents digging pinecones out of the snow for fuel, Vikin cut my father in on his business selling black-market silk and cigarette lighters to the prostitutes around Innsbruck, who alone seemed to have a bit of money to spend. My father would remember their partnership fondly: the deep, frozen nights with the snowfields of the Hafelekarspitze still glowing pink high above the town; the pleasure of making a few shillings at a time when money mattered a great deal, the half-serious bargaining with the ladies, who weren't opposed to barter.

If Vikin admired my mother, as I'm convinced he did, he kept it to himself. The two of them would talk about everything— where they hoped to go, what life might bring them. When my mother contracted scarlet fever, he took over whenever my father had to be away, scrounging medicine or food; later, during her convalescence, he'd spend days lying on the floor by her mattress, propped on an elbow, joking with her, smoking, playing endless games of Old Maid. It didn't go unnoticed. Increasingly worried for their safety, my parents' friends tried to talk some sense into them: What was the matter with them—didn't they realize who they were dealing with? It was only a matter of time before he turned. Unable to believe it, my parents put them off. Understanding the situation, Vikin, like a tactful ghost, began appearing only after those who feared him had gone.

The day my parents told him their good news, that they'd secured passage on a ship to Australia, that they'd be leaving for Naples in five days, Vikin couldn't speak. For a second, my father said, his rough, handsome face looked like a mask. He rallied instantly, mumbled how happy he was for them, then left soon afterward.

Two days before their departure, Vikin disappeared. The hours wound down. My parents asked around but no one had seen him. They didn't know what had happened. Had the thought of having to say goodbye been too much for him? Did he think they were abandoning him? Had he cut himself off to spare himself the grief? Or to punish them for leaving? They'd been friends. They'd hoped to say goodbye.

There was nothing to do. The hour came to leave for the station—no Vikin. Perhaps he'd be waiting for them there—he knew the time of their departure. He wasn't. A big, milling crowd, friends seeing off friends. There was still time—fifteen minutes, a little less—maybe he'd make it at the last minute.

He didn't. The train—a refugee transport with hard plank benches—came into the station and they pushed their way on. Ten minutes later the conductor stepped up, the whistle blew, the train lurched and began to move. My parents stood leaning out the lowered window, waving to their few friends, still scanning the crowd for the one face they'd hoped to see. It wasn't there. The train gathered speed.

And then he was there, bursting through the crowd like a rugby player, sprinting down the platform, his coat billowing behind him. Losing ground, he managed to hand off a huge, mounded basket to a man three cars down along with a threat that he'd hunt him down and cut his throat if he learned that the basket hadn't reached its intended party—the lady in the red jacket, three cars down.

The basket, an impossible treasure trove of my mother's favorite foods—pâté and apricot jam and pickles—a virtual inventory of all the things she'd mentioned, daydreaming, over the course of those five hundred days, reached its intended party. They never saw or heard of Vikin again.

I always loved that story. It's only now, writing it down, that I think I see it for what it is. The one-name card sharp with the heart of gold? That last-second cinematic entrance? It's fiction—a story embedded in fact, embellished over time.

But if I don't quite believe in Vikin—at least not the one in the story—how is it possible for me to see him? Because I do. What kind of "seeing" allows me to imagine a man I never met, never spoke to, and don't completely believe existed?

He bursts from the crowd like a rugby player, hurtles a suitcase, sprints down the platform. I can see the billowing coat, the strain in his face, see him, at full speed, handing the basket up to the window. He's part of my legacy now, my store of memories—I'll remember his run the rest of my life, dream it when I'm old.

XXXV

TELLING ANY STORY INVOLVES sacrificing some things for others, thinning the row. Hardly news. What surprises me this time, though, is how hard I find it. I always enjoyed cutting back, opening up silences, always agreed with Hemingway that pretty much any story could be made better by being made shorter. The problem is, when it comes to my parents' story, it doesn't feel like I'm paring a manuscript, it feels like I'm paring a life, and the ellipses, the omissions, seem like lies.

It can't be helped. I have to stick to the trail of my story or risk losing myself in a wilderness of "facts"—fake trees, remembered valleys, rivers more rumor than truth. I know this, but it doesn't sit easy. What gives me the right to cut ahead, to leave out faces, years—all for the sake of the *one* narrative, the one face, that I've decided shaped them all? By what authority do I get to decide?

The answer is brutal, unarguable—something like an essential human right: By the authority of survival, which bestows on us all the right to shape until we are shaped in turn. It's a dangerous authority, an imprimatur that can tempt to arrogance—after all, those who would catch or correct me are gone—but I'll take it. It's my turn now. It's my story. I'll write what I believe, cut what I want.

I sound defensive. I know why.

In the bad years, let's say between the Bee Gees' "Stayin' Alive" and Hall and Oates' "Maneater," when my mother was going crazy in our little suburban house in Pennsylvania and my father was barely hangin' on to his shit, as the children say, I'd come home from college on the weekends and the three of us would talk. It didn't feel like a choice. During the week I'd rehearse excuses for why I couldn't make it, but Friday would always find me, duffel bag on my shoulder, on the No. 1 subway to Port Authority, where I'd catch the Allentown bus to the Holiday Inn off Route 22. From the green lights of the Holiday Inn, I'd walk the two miles in the dark—a bit less if I cut through the cornfields—to our house. They were all alone, and that house was the most silent house in the world. I had to do what I could.

And so we'd talk over slices of my mother's bábovka (she still baked then) and endless cups of tea. We'd talk for hours, sitting in that narrow living room with the beige sofa and the overvar-nished, slice-of-a-tree coffee table and the crackling leatherette recliner that you moved back with a kind of stick shift on the right-hand side, and sometimes it would go well and we'd talk about school and politics and books, reminisce and laugh while our cat, Chiquita, slept on her embroidered cushion, once maroon, now the color of dried blood, and sometimes it wouldn't.

There were different ways for it not to go well, but one in particular stands out. It would work like this: Over the course of a two-or-three-hour conversation, the talk would drift from this to that, from—I don't know—Jimmy Carter to peanuts to whomever I might be dating (always a dangerous subject) to some remembered day ("Do you remember that time we . . . ?"), and somewhere along the way we'd get into a long argument about, say, whether vitamins made sense or were just a lot of hype. We'd talk about it for fifteen, twenty minutes or more, marshaling arguments, coming up with (probably bogus) evidence, maintaining this side or that . . . who cares?—the point is that we'd spend a long time talking about vitamins, and then, eventually, the conversation would jump to something else.

Maybe half an hour later, seeing some kind of connection, I might say, "But isn't that just like the thing with the vitamins?" and my mother would look at me and say, "What vitamins?"

This is how it would start.

"You know, the vitamins," I'd say—"about whether they're a scam and all that."

My mother would shrug uncomprehendingly: "I have no idea what you're talking about."

"I'm talking about vitamins," I'd say, and laugh, "you know, that whole argument we just had about—"

"Why would we have an argument?"

"Fine, not an argument, a conversation—"

"Why are you so upset?"

"I'm not upset, I'm just . . . I just don't see how you can't remember that."

"Do *you* have any idea what he's talking about?" she'd say to my father.

My father would shake his head.

By now I wouldn't be laughing. "I'm talking about vitamins," I'd say, confused, "about the long conversation the three of us had just a few seconds ago—"

"A few seconds ago?"

"Minutes ago—"

"You just said seconds—"

"—in this room, in which you said . . ."

"I don't understand why this means so much to you."

"It doesn't, I'm just saying . . . For Christ's sake, just five minutes ago you . . ." And I'd go on to recount big chunks of the conversation: what my father had said, how my mother had made the point, let's say, that in the old days *her* mother simply cooked what she cooked and you ate what was put in front of you and were grateful for it . . . How could they not remember this? Why would I make it up?

And my mother would pause, then look at me and say, very calmly, as if gentling a horse, "Nobody's said a word about vitamins all day," then turn to my father. "Did *you* hear anyone say anything about vitamins?" and they'd both shake their heads and my mother would say, *Kluk má nervy na dranc*—something like, "The boy's nerves are shot" but closer to "He's losing it"—and exchange worried looks, then awkwardly change the subject. And that would be that. If I chose to pursue it—and I would—there'd be a fight. I'd lose.

It didn't happen often, true—then again, with some things a

little goes a long way. I had no tape to play back, no brothers or sisters or eccentric old aunts to confirm what I remembered. It was just the three of us. It was always just the three of us. I couldn't understand what was going on—why would they do this? I could recall specific details of what we'd said, who'd answered whom— how was it possible they didn't remember? And then there'd be that look—a look that those with mental handicaps must know very well—a look that moves from worried confusion (a gathering between the eyebrows) to comprehension (a spasm, like gas), to embarrassment (a certain tightness, the cheekbones standing out, then a quick glance away), to a lame attempt to cover up (often betrayed by a slight, almost involuntary shake of the head).

It seemed so sincere—*was* so sincere—that it threw me. After all, how could I be so sure? Was it possible that I'd imagined it all? Could there be something wrong with me? After all, this was my mom and dad—why would they lie? What right did I have to disregard what they both remembered, or, rather, *didn't* remember? By what authority could *my* memory, *my* truth, override theirs?

It seems ridiculous to me now, all this adolescent angst— irritating in that special, almost parental way that our younger selves are often irritating to us. I'm disappointed in me; I should have been tougher, smarter. I'm like one of those fathers in their wrinkled office shirts stalking around the edge of the wrestling circle yelling, "Put him down, goddamn it! Show some guts!" I'm just glad my nineteen-year-old self can't hear me, because he'd get up off the couch, wipe the tears of frustration off his face with the back of his wrists and punch me in the face.

The fact is, it mattered then. It mattered because I loved

them, and because love—more than is generally acknowledged, I think—is about trust. If I was weak, then I was weak, but I've never been able to laugh at the concessions that love can wring from us. After all, this wasn't just another argument about "young people these days" or the general decline of music since Mozart. This was an ontological battle. As the joke went, "Who you gonna believe—me, or your lyin' eyes?" I had to choose who to believe, and one way or the other there'd be blood on the floor.

It wouldn't be mine. Not this time.

Nothing happened. I just never trusted them quite the same way again. Though I'd return to Bethlehem for years (and backslide into loving them for decades), the moment that I decided that nothing, not even love, trumped the sanctity of my own consciousness, I simultaneously left home and became a writer. I'd manage to run from both facts for twelve years—I'm good at running—but it didn't matter: the bearing had hit.

It's as good a creation myth as any.

Forty years later, our beige sofa sits rotting in my mother's overgrown villa in the tiny, medieval village of Zadní Vydří in Moravia. The carnival's moved on: Our house in Bethlehem has been someone else's burden for a generation. My father's gone and my mother just about, and last summer, going through my mother's moldering rooms at Vydří, I found a flat, colorless mat under a pile of water-damaged books and recognized it as the embroidered cushion that Chiquita used to sleep on. Sentimental fool that I am, I couldn't bring myself to throw it out.

Like turtles crossing a highway to get to water, we'll do what we have to do to be. When I think of the three of us in that dark little house, Eddie Albert crooning "Make the World Go Away" from the windowless dining room, I'm struck by the dumb, vine-like strength of a kid's trust. That trust was like life itself—even as it looped around my throat. It took an act of violence to cut it.

It would take some years for me to understand that that's what liberation sometimes demands.

That's my authority.

XXXVI

IT'S SUMMER, 1949. PEE Wee Hunt's "Twelfth Street Rag" is a big hit, the Berlin blockade has ended, the Stalinist show trials are in full swing. My parents, twenty-six and twenty-four years old, are on the transport train to Naples. As for me, I'm still in the great dark—a prelife ghost.

I need to speed the clock, make the calendar pages flutter. I need to get to where the answers lie and the story resumes, and if that involves putting history in the microwave, in it goes. A chapter should do it.

Picture those corny white dashes from the opening of *Casablanca*, that toy plane crossing the Mediterranean, that hectoring narrator's voice, so suited for peddling Geritol. . . . *And so, a torturous, round-about refugee trail sprang up. Paris to Marseilles, across the Mediterranean to Oran . . .*

I love that movie for many reasons, but one of the most important is that the world it depicts—the world of Rick and Ilsa and Victor Laszlo, Ilsa's rectitudinal Czech-o-slo-vakian husband with the oddly Hungarian surname (the *a* in "slovakian" always pronounced in the horrible nasal of "back-*pack*" rather than "tick-*tock*")—was my parents' reality. Sort of. Fine, hardly at all. Not, basically. Still.

I like to imagine them selling the real *Casablanca*, or the post-war version, at any rate: Prod the MGM roaring lion, hoist up the Warner Brothers' shield: "Coming Soon to a Theatre Near *You*! An Unforgettable Story of Tedium and Uncertainty, Recrimination and Regret . . ."

It would be a tricky thing to score. Instead of the chorus of *"La Marseillaise"* conducted by Laszlo for Major Strasser's benefit, you'd want to go for something less obvious, less rousing; something closer in spirit to Kafka than Capra (or Curtiz, for that matter): Satie's *Fourth Gnossienne*, maybe, or a cut from *Sylvester and Tweety*—a whistle, a slap, a vibrating spring. The absurd was everywhere, and wherever it was, as Sylvester could tell you, pain wasn't far behind.

On July 21, 1949—a kind of Sylvester moment—my parents waited for five hours on the docks of Sydney Harbor in a long, wilting line of "New Australians," waiting to be "processed." Ahead of them, a former professor of engineering from Budapest who they'd gotten to know came forward and placed his one bag, a pillowcase, on the long, wooden table for inspection: a single pair of shoes, rubber-banded together sole to sole, three books tied with string to keep them from getting damaged, two shirts wrapped in paper, one cap, one small book of photographs, one raincoat, one can opener. When the young man calling out the list of items pulled out a heavy steel pipe with wires extending from both ends, everything stopped.

The professor started to explain—in Hungarian, alas—but was politely asked to take a step back. A higher-up was summoned. What the bloody hell was this? A pipe with wires coming out of it, its ends crudely blocked to hold them in place? Another official was called.

Summoning his few words of English, the professor tried again—"Is no problem, yes?"—then switched to flawed but serviceable German: *Entschuldigen Sie mich, bitte—das ist nur meine*. . . . A raised finger from the officials—"Quiet please. Wait!" At this point my mother, who spoke both German and English, stepped forward and offered to interpret. "Madam, you will return to your place in line." She returned to her place in line.

This went on for some time. Frustrated, people began to grumble, then call out. An official was prying at one of the stoppers with a pocket knife—his companions had stepped back—gingerly working it from side to side. When it slipped out, he carefully held the pipe up to his eye. Nothing. Again my mother offered to interpret—she had no idea what the thing was, either—and again was asked to kindly not interfere. The most recent wave of DPs (Displaced Persons) had been described that very morning in *The Sun* as generally "the worst types," that is, Nazis, Communists, gangsters and prostitutes; they were all the same, and the man hadn't helped his case by speaking German.

Perhaps a half-hour in, the professor abruptly bent and took off his shoes. No one noticed. When he took off his pants— apparently having gone quite mad—they noticed. Officials started yelling, waving their arms. Clamping his pants' legs to his chest with his chin, the professor folded them neatly along the seam, walked over to the dumbstruck officials in his underwear and, grasping the ends of the wires in his hand, draped his pants over his makeshift clothes hanger. He had only the one pair. He needed to take care of them.

Though hardly a knee-slapper, the scene might be worth a small smile—the bumbling officials, nervous about detonating a clothes hanger, the wacky professor standing in his bloomers, folding his pants—*until*, that is, you consider that this was a time when men and women were less inclined to make spectacles of themselves in public (or in front of the camera), a time when an accomplished man, respected in his work—who may or may not have lost his family but who'd most certainly lost everything else, and who now found himself starting over in a new country whose language he didn't speak with nothing more than a pillowcase of possessions to his name—might actually be humiliated by his poverty, his skinny white legs, the depth to which he'd fallen. Factor that in, and the chuckle dies—or should.

And yet—admit it!—it's hard to *feel*—after all, it's not you. Or me, for that matter.

The thing is, it wasn't them, either—until it was. Which is how it always goes. One day you're coming home from the office, throwing your keys on the table, yelling up the stairs to your kids that dinner's almost ready. You have a nice house, a decent salary, security, friends, enough contentment to actually realize—in short, unsustainable bursts—exactly how happy you are. Two years later you're alone, hand-washing your underwear in a sink, then hanging it on the wire you've strung between the metal poles of your bunk bed. You're somewhere else. Everything is gone. When you wake at night, it takes you a while to remember. There are guards, fences. Your credentials mean nothing. You own nothing. You *are* nothing. Everyone speaks Pashto, and when you don't understand, they speak louder or gesticulate like you're a fool. You're an imposition, a burden, pitied if you're lucky. You barely recognize yourself. Your country—where only yesterday you were coming home to your family, throwing your keys on the table—doesn't exist anymore: It's someone else's country now. You may be able to go back in your lifetime. You may not.

Feel it now? Just a little?

What I'm trying to say is that the late 1940s—like all times marked by massive refugee migrations, like the summer and fall of 2015, for example—were a time of bewilderment and displacement and fear. There were some who had an easier time of it—people with money and connections, or high-ranking Nazis fortunate enough to be spirited to safety by the Catholic Church or an American government eager to recruit former enemies to the Cold War cause—but the vast majority were just faces caught in a riptide of sweating men in hats and women in calf-length skirts filling out displaced-persons forms, peeling potatoes into a pot, hanging sheets over curtainless windows in Toronto and Buenos Aires and Brisbane. Surgeons emptied bedpans; scholars scoured the insides of industrial pipe in the heat. These people weren't one thing or another, but almost without exception, whatever they'd been before, they weren't any more. Some fought that truth, others welcomed it. It depended on the ghosts they brought with them. It depended on their nature, their tendency to mourn or move.

My parents, who hadn't really been anywhere before, were part of that tide, swept from place to place, sleeping when and where they could. Two and a half days after leaving Innsbruck (I can see them sitting side by side on the wooden planks, doling out the luxuries from Vikin's basket), their train arrived in Naples, Vesuvius smoking dramatically in the distance, where cordons of machine-gun–carrying *carabinieri* funneled them onto open-bed trucks. Escorted by police, the trucks took them—standing up, hanging on to the metal tarp scaffolding—to Camp Bagnoli, a fenced-in holding facility where 8,000 refugees lived for the mornings when the numbers of those scheduled for departure were posted in the administration building. My mother and father, segregated into men's and women's buildings (a third set of dormitories was reserved for mothers with children), were displaced persons #758 and #759.

They scrounged, hustled, made alliances where they could, trying, like all refugees, to keep their footing in a world careening between the farcical and the frightening. When the quarter-rations of food—weak coffee smelling of beets, a dollop of spaghetti for dinner—began to take their toll on my mother's health, my father managed to talk one of the camp police (a Czech basketball star who'd been given the position in exchange for playing for the Bagnoli team) into looking the other way long enough for him to make it out to the local town after dark where, in forty minutes, without a word of Italian, he managed to sell his watch for a fistful of lire, two salamis and a bag of oranges.

Bizarrely, my parents would remember the hour my father was gone as worse, in many ways, than the time on the train in Vienna. They couldn't explain it. If my father had been caught—and the odds were high he would be, given the police presence in the local towns and the fact that he stuck out like a donkey in a kennel— he'd have been arrested, tried, imprisoned. But it wasn't that, they said. It was because, having made it this far, the thought of being separated was more than they could bear.

More than forty years have passed since they said those words to me—*as if being separated was more than we could bear*—and though I know that people come together and go their way, I still don't understand by what route, what slow accretion of resentment and pain, you get from wanting nothing more than to be allowed to continue on together, to sitting in some lawyer's office in Christmas City, USA—*And one more signature if you don't mind, here, and here*—doing to yourself what you'd once feared would be done unto you by others. Is there nothing that the passage of time can't dissolve?—though just this instant, writing this, I mistyped "dissolve" as "disslove" and stumbled into what I didn't know I wanted to say.

My father made it back with the lire, the salamis, the oranges. The basketball star from Nedvedice closed up the fence. The lawyer's office would have to wait another forty-two years.

They went on. They'd be lucky. Less than a month after entering Camp Bagnoli, they'd make the reverse trip—again escorted by armed *carabinieri*, Vesuvius still smoking—to the Port of

Naples where they'd board the USS *General Harry Taylor*, one of the so-called Liberty ships that the United States had stamped out at the rate of two ships a day for four years, effectively burying the Axis powers.

The irony of troop ships ferrying refugees from the war they'd helped win was probably lost on no one; still, there were richer ironies to be savored. Of these, one stands out, a freak of history.

There are times when the truth outruns us all.

Among the Polish laborers and Romanian musicians and Czech journalists on board the Liberty ships, a certain percentage also happened to be graduates of Treblinka and Majdanek; that is, human beings—some more scarred than others—who'd made it through the fire and begun the lifelong work of regaining their lives, only to be displaced again. People like our friends the Horners, who hadn't met my parents yet (or even each other, for that matter), but who would find themselves sitting on our porch at Twin Lakes with their two boys in the summer of 1970, having just come in from a swim.

People who'd survived what should, by rights, be unimaginable.

For a long time I didn't register that camp survivors had been among the displaced—though how that's possible, given the people we knew when I was young, I don't know. I think on some level I still believed that suffering confers special benefits, immunity from future injustices; that having survived Buchenwald, you were done.

I was wrong. Mixed in with camp survivors like the Horner

were men who, reaching to wash their backs in the communal show-ers, would inadvertently reveal the small, SS blood group tattoo (on the white skin of the inner arm, just below the armpit) which, as my father put it, explained their eagerness to emigrate and proved, yet again, that past crimes don't disqualify us from future opportunities.

I've tried to imagine that moment, that moment when each recognized the other's tattoo, but it's a black hole to me—a moment so dense with context it seems impossible. There you are, naked, stripped of your prisoners' garb, your black SS uniform—everything but your history. It's a continent glimpsed through a keyhole.

And I keep wondering: At that moment, who feared who more?

We never asked. Some moments are yours to bury.

XXXVII

I DON'T BELIEVE SHE ever stopped thinking about him. Ever. Even now, if anything survives, it's some vision of him—his face, his voice, his body. I believe that. I'd wish it for her. I never begrudged her that love.

I don't think my mother's memories of F. kept her—particularly in those early years in Innsbruck, in Sydney, later in Munich—from caring for my father. I think she did care for him. I think they cared for each other, in fact, that they "made a pretty good team" (to recall *The Graduate*), but that from the very beginning they were like magnets robbed of their electric charge; I don't remember ever coming home—as my friends did—to that inexplicable good mood, to contented smiles and whispers in the kitchen.

Speculating about our parents' sex life always feels a bit disingenuous—it seems so, well, *unlikely* (though here we are to prove it). In my case, two photographs speak the proverbial two thousand words—or a hundred, anyway. In both—the first taken on a dock on the Weltersee in Germany, the second somewhere in Sydney in the early 1950s—my mother and father are with a different friend. Both men were part of the refugee migration to Australia and eventually the New World—men I knew and cared for.

I love those photographs—the morning stillness of the first, the big-city vibe of the second, the way my father leans forward on that dock in Germany, eager to go, to see—but that's not what matters most. What matters most, at least to me, is that in both pictures (and a dozen like them) my mother is subtly leaning away from my father and toward the other man exactly as if, to charge my earlier metaphor, she and my father were opposing poles of a magnet. They're husband and wife, yet there's no hand on the knee, no arm around the waist, no draw, no pull, no valence. It's a visual metaphor of their bedroom.

It's a miracle I'm here.

I suppose it's possible to overstate the role that sex plays in our lives, but it takes effort. How much did sex—or the lack of it—actually matter? I think in my parents' case it mattered a lot, that the weather in our house always came from the bedroom; that even early on, years before things got really bad, it was an issue between them. Thrown into a marriage mined by abuse, triggered to explode, they were never able to get it right, and whatever affection there may have been between them only made it worse, turning closeness into a taunt.

The lack of physical attraction between a couple can be a brutal thing, and the road to just-friendship traverses a crevasse.

That my mother and father never made that crossing suggests

(just to flog my exhausted metaphor another mile down the road) that the *lack* of charge between them may not have been the problem after all; if it had been, the transition to some comfortable coexistence in backless slippers would have been easy. Instead, they tortured each other (and themselves), my mother buying lingerie to inspire a man she didn't want and regularly ridiculed, my father fighting back by not seeing her, by choking off whatever desire he may have had for her, by rolling over and going to sleep for days, then months, then years.

On those nights when I was three, or four, when, troubled by nightmares, I'd be allowed to sleep between them (tunneling down into their warmth, the tears wet on my face, endlessly safe), I didn't know I was doing them a favor.

I'm tempted to say that the way they were together explained the other man. It would make sense. That a lack—whatever its source—created a need. And I might just go with that if I didn't know how it was.

How it was suggested something more than a physical need, which I suppose any number of men could have satisfied in a pinch. How it was suggested something much bigger: an absence generating a dream—a dream of salvation, of deliverance—which then came to be embodied in a single human being. It was as if all the problems in my mother's life, all the pain—psychological, physical, spiritual—had one solution. A ridiculous idea. Except that it happened to be true.

For weeks and months at a time after they arrived in Australia, my parents lived separately—not because they wanted to, but because they had to go wherever they were assigned work. While my mother lived in a dormitory room in a Surry Hills hospital, for example, my father slept in a tent city outside the ironworks in Chullora, shoveling coal with a concert oboist from Prague. While my mother mopped floors and cleaned toilets ten hours a day in Sydney, my father cut sugarcane in Queensland where, by ten in the morning, the workers would be encased in a dripping glaze of sugar and sweat like strips of human fly paper. Wasps drowned on their skin.

For much of that first year in Australia, my mother received letters from F. and wrote to him in turn. How instantly her week must have been tranformed on seeing the thin, blue *luftpost* envelope on her bunk. What extrordinarily blissful games she must have played with herself before she opened it, saving it, suffering, ecstatic, till after she'd washed up, till after supper, till after everyone was asleep. . . .

I don't know how it happened. I'll never know how he found her—Czechoslovakia was a rapidly closing door, and there were no directories of "political subversives tried in absentia and found guilty of crimes against the state." What address could she have given him, considering how much she moved? How could *her* letters have made it back to him without putting him in danger with the secret police?

All I know is that they managed it, somehow. That they wrote to each other for months. That his letters were indescribably precious to her—something she secreted away in books and under the lining of hat boxes for forty years. I know this because she showed them to me, a tight, blue packet taped to the back of one of her dresser drawers, one rainy morning in Bethlehem when I was sixteen.

I never read them. She never offered and I never asked. I knew they existed—that was enough. That she'd trusted me with her secret.

I also know that at some point in 1949 or 1950 the letters had stopped coming.

It must have been excruciating, that waiting, the dialogue in your head so incessant at first that you barely notice mopping another hallway, scrubbing another toilet, one voice whispering "Something's wrong, something's happened," the other rationalizing, excusing, calculating dates, saying, "It's only been three weeks," "maybe he had the flu," "maybe it was lost in the mail," and then the weeks become months and four of your letters have gone unanswered and the hallways are endless and quiet, the toilets innumerable, your arms, your legs—but why not say it?—your heart so heavy you can barely move.

And there comes that point when, having written everything that can be written—keeping it light at first, eventually pleading for an answer, for clarity, for anything at all—you stop. Because there's nothing more to do. Because he's obviously faced reality, moved on. Because you're married and 10,000 miles away. Because you never gave him hope, not really. Because you couldn't see any hope to give—and he'd understood what you weren't saying.

And life resumes, because it has to. Because it has its own plans. My father's there now—he has a job stringing Wilson tennis rackets. You work decent hours in the Sydney Library. The two of you have a small apartment that you've painted white, even something of a community. You'll remember this. You'll have stories to tell: of your friend, Vera, who opened a phone booth in Surry Hills to ask a man if he'd be much longer only to have him crash to the sidewalk with a knife in his ribs; of the shark sirens going off on Bondi Beach, the young lifeguards charging into the surf on their boards, deliberately putting themselves in harm's way; of the cockaburras that would alight on perambulators and peck out the eyes of infants left unattended, of inch-long soldier ants that would rear up on their hind legs in the dirt and challenge your passing. Life would move on, your heart would sleep. And it wouldn't all be one thing—there'd be good times, too, nights of laughter and singing with friends, and that overcast New Year's Day when this man that you'd married, who you'd rather come to like—maybe even love?—said something to you on the beach, teasing you, and you scooped water into your bathing cap and ran after him down the sand past the Aussies with their heads propped on the bottoms of beer bottles like so many golf balls on cues.

And maybe you thought of him as the seasons passed—of what had happened to him, of what could have gone wrong—remembered his voice, his face, the way you were together . . . and maybe you didn't. There was nothing to do—the heart had to sleep.

And months turn to years and you leave Australia and return to Europe where you live for a while in a dank, beautiful house outside Munich, then sail to New York—the Statue of Liberty emerging from the fog, the city skyline looming white in the morning sun like cliffs in a dream—and six years pass and McCarthy's long gone and Sputnik's been launched and it's January 28, 1958, a night of heavy snow, and lying in a hospital bed in Queens, exhausted, cramping, you write in a small blue diary, "A little boy was born to us today. . . ."

And you breathe him in like a second life. He'll be the world made right. He'll be your friend, your soul mate, the one you trust above anyone on earth. He'll be everything you're not.

The world rushes on. It won't leave you alone. Khrushchev pounds his shoe and the world holds its breath and then your mother's gone and Kennedy's been shot and your father's coming to New York to visit and the river runs faster through Berlin and Selma and on to Vietnam, from *Will you still need me?* to the Summer of Love, and Alexander Dubček's reforms are holding and they're calling it the Prague Spring and for a moment, just one moment, everything seems possible and then it's summer and you're at the cabin at Lost Lake watching the tanks enter Prague on the news and nothing is. And life begins to close in.

It's so hard to hold on to it. Everything breaks. Things start off well, then fail you, betray you. Your love, your trust. It's always like that. Everything's like that. If only you could sleep, rest; if only you could hold on, but life slips through your fingers, willfully, maliciously, running away from you. But you still have your boy—by God, you have that. He's changed, of course, though that's to be expected, and he spends evenings in his room reading *Field & Stream* and lately he's been picking up things at that school of his because he's begun talking back, even accusing you of things in a tone of voice you've never heard from him before, with this look, deliberately pushing you, testing you, but he doesn't know you—you have your limits—and when you grabbed him by the collar the other day like your mother would have if you'd ever dared talk to *her* like that and washed out his mouth with soap (though the bar was too big to fit in his mouth, which was awkward), it seemed to have some effect. Because he's a good boy, really—my God what a sweet child he was. There's no one in the world you trust more.

That boy, Jan Palach, who immolated himself on Wenceslas Square to protest the invasion—what must that be like?

Sometimes you feel like that dog, Laika, that the Soviets sent into space. Circling till you die.

But you still have your boy. He's a good boy—you used to laugh so much together. People say he looks just like you.

This summer in Connecticut will do you all some good.

XXXVIII

LOOKING BACK ON OUR lives everything appears foreordained, a series of amazing coincidences leading us unerringly to where we are. No discussion, no debate. It's a form of tyranny, no more legitimate than the divine right of kings. The sceptered present— sanctioned, no, *sanctified*, by what is—lords it over the past, and we bow down and pay fealty: After all, how could it have been otherwise, since it wasn't? But apply just a light wash of imagination and the narrative quivers, branches, flowers into the million ways it might have gone.

The past conditional tense is the only time machine I know. And the seedbed of all regret.

What would have changed if my mother had known, say, twenty-five years earlier than she did, that F.'s letters had stopped coming *not* because he'd forgotten her but because *her* letters had stopped coming to him—because she'd obviously moved on, started a new life with her husband, forgotten. If she'd known in 1950, or 1952, that he'd continued writing to her for months, keeping it light at first, then growing desperate, finally asking for nothing more than an answer, clarity, anything. Eventually shutting it down, moving on, because there was nothing else to do.

It would be another twelve years before F. would learn that his father, disapproving of the affair, had intercepted my mother's letters to him while at the same time generously offering to post his—and burning them instead.

By then he'd be married, with two sons of his own.

It could have gone differently. It didn't.

There's a footnote.

In 1966, not long after John Lennon declared the Beatles "more popular than Jesus," F. found himself appointed to a delegation of engineers traveling to New York. The forty-one-year-old former Green Beret from Žďár had done well for himself, and the authorities in charge of denying exit visas had deemed him a safe bet: with a wife and two sons staying behind in Czechoslovakia (the secret police dossier described the marriage as flawed, but his relation to the boys a strong one), the chances of defection were slim.

What the powers-that-be couldn't have known was that the chief engineer had heard a rumor that my parents had emigrated to New York. That he'd called in every favor he had to be sent abroad. That once in the city he'd go off the reservation—risking his career, possibly even his freedom—to look for my mother.

Ten days are a long time to search for someone you haven't

seen in eighteen years—someone who's married (as you are), who has children (as you do), someone who, for all you know, may not want to see you, or worse, may greet you with that "Oh, my goodness, well this *is* a surprise" distance that tells you it's dead and never coming back.

It would have been natural for him to falter, to wake up to the insanity of it, to allow reason to gently take him by the hand and lead him back to the conference room.

Apparently, faltering wasn't in the man's nature. For ten days he made phone calls, followed leads, pushed on with a few phrases of English and a pocket dictionary. And then he had it: our address in Rego Park, Queens. He found the IND subway, dropped the token in the slot.

A rainy April morning, the loaf-shaped hedges beginning to green. No one was home. The super was out. He waited outside the building, leaning against the glass doors, smoking, then went back inside and left a note with his phone number at the hotel, and another one, for the super, which he worked out with the dictionary. Both went unanswered.

That evening, someone named Rosenfeld or Falconetti or Kabata would find an incomprehensible note (Was it Polish?) on the door of their new apartment on 63rd Road in Queens. Less than half an hour away, meanwhile, my mother was unpacking cartons marked KITCHEN in our new house in Ardsley. Our new number wasn't listed in the phone books yet.

He didn't find her. Time ran out. The delegation, including the disgraced chief engineer, returned to John F. Kennedy Airport. There would be questions to answer in Prague; the event would go into his file. It would take years to make up for the transgression. I don't believe he regretted it.

It's 1966, a rainy April morning. My mother's making *bábovka* in the new kitchen, fluffing up the heavy batter with a wooden ladle. I'm in my room, pretending to write a report on volcanoes while secretly studying the picture from the Garcia Fishing Catalog of the man rearing back on his rod, desperately tightening the star drag on his blood-red, Abu Matic 170 Spincasting Reel as a thirty-pound musky thrashes in the foreground. My father's at the auto repair in Dobbs Ferry getting ripped off by George, who he thinks is his friend.

"*Kluku, maš hlad?*" my mother calls from the kitchen—Hey, kiddo, you hungry? "*Chceš něco k—*" You want something to—?

And the doorbell rings, and my mother pushes her hair back with her forearm, dusts the flour off her hands, and goes to answer it.

XXXIX

HER LAUGHTER COULD BE SO wonderful, so child-like—snorting
and gasping for air, *Oh, God, please, stop, enough*—that it would
just sweep everything before it. I remember it so well. Eventually it
retreated somewhere inside of her, but every now and then I'd still
hear it, or some echo of it, and whenever I did, especially in the later
years when she seemed like a guttering candle, for that second I'd
see her again, waving to me from inside the tower.

Let me tell you about my mother.

Sometimes when I watched *Daniel Boone* on TV—I had
green, high-top Daniel Boone sneakers and regularly busted my
father's axes throwing them against trees like Fess Parker, then
burying the parts in the woods—she'd make me *palačinky* for
dinner: Czech crepes so light and thin you could tell if the jam
inside them was apricot or raspberry. I'd eat them one by one,
draping them over my thumb and pinky while Dan'l and his side-
kick Mingo fought off another Cherokee war party or split dead
trees with axes that didn't break, and in those moments I'd be so
happy I couldn't sit still and she'd take one of the *palačinky* for

herself and watch *Daniel Boone* with me and everything would be perfect.

She loved to sing, and she knew more verses to more Czech folk songs—and could sing them later into the night, accompanied by violins and guitars and our friends' disbelieving laughter—than anyone who ever lived.

She'd get a kick out of dumb pranks—the water balloon perched above the door, the legs unscrewed off the chair, the forty-pound snapping turtle with the griffin claws that we hid in the steamer trunk in the living room of our cabin that hissed and lunged like a locomotive when our friends put down their drinks.

One early summer morning when I was ten, we were reading on plastic deck chairs in the garden when she suddenly went inside the cabin, returned with a ball of string and rigged up a kind of clothesline so that it ran just in front of our faces, an easy arm's reach away. She hung the line with bunches of grapes, and we spent the afternoon reclining like Roman senators on our plastic deck chairs, reading and plucking the fat muscatels like low-hanging fruit.

When I was sixteen and sad for some reason, she swept me up and the two of us drove out to the mountains of western Pennsylvania, where I took a fourteen-mile run through a narrow river valley at dusk, the chill, October air smelling of wet leaves and water, the evening star like a pinhole in the blue, then returned to our creaky wooden hotel for dinner. We talked about everything that evening, and the next day, and the one after that. She was my best friend. It was the last good trip we had.

She had the complicated gift of compassion, of understanding others' pain.

She loved Brook Benton's "Rainy Night in Georgia," and the Beatles' "Yesterday," and Simon and Garfunkel's "Bridge over Troubled Water."

Later, she also loved Helen Reddy's "You and Me Against the World," which ends, God have mercy on us all, with a child's voice chirping "I love you, Mommy," and Helen answering "I love you too, baby."

She took great pride in "not letting herself go," hunted for designer dresses in the thrift shops on 2nd Avenue, did exercises with Jack LaLanne—*And ten more, ladies!*—who, in his black jump suit, biceps a-bulgin', always looked to me like one of those action figures you could twist so their feet stuck out of their armpits.

This is like trying to build a hawk out of wire and wood.

Fuck Jack LaLanne.

Let me tell you about my mother.

These aren't facts—they're truths:

My mother loved me when I was young, in that bone-of-my-bone, flesh-of-my-flesh kind of way which leads so easily to betrayal.

She came to hate me as I grew older—you could see it in her face, hear it in her voice—which was like watching someone you love draw a razor down their arm to hurt you.

There are harder things than being hated by someone who loved you once and not knowing why, but not many.

I hear her inside of me. I always will. Both of "her"—the person "before" and the person "after." The mother who held me, and the one whose rage sprayed my face with spittle.

I hear them both.

And I fly from anger to love like a kid on a swing.

When I was nineteen, I read *Moby-Dick* in a thirteenth-floor dormitory room where I'd gone to escape my home. The building was nearly empty. I read at night while blizzards swept in over the Hudson, rattling the windows. And I remember being brought to tears by "crazy" Ahab, as much by his iron indomitability—"Speak not to me of blasphemy, man; I'd strike the sun if it insulted me!"—as by his one moment of vulnerability when, moved by the inexplicable scent of grass on the air, he pictures mowers resting in the shade of the Andes, and weeps.

My mother loved the world—deeply, desperately—and the world betrayed her. She never forgave it.

XL

It was Bethlehem that finished her. Bethlehem with its self-righteous thumb up its ass, its Presbyterian propriety, its sexlessness and silence. I've never hated a place more.

We lived at 3452 Lord Byron Drive (which suggests at least 3,000 other sad little ranch houses like ours), just off Chaucer and Walt Whitman Lane, surrounded by miles of cornfields—snowy stubble half the year, stifling monocrop the other—that children never played in. Of course, it wasn't Bethlehem alone; Bethlehem just made it easy to pretend it was.

Could another family have been happy there? I have no doubt they could (though I've always sensed a terrible loneliness in these American spaces carved overnight out of meadows and woods, then named after nineteenth-century poets or Ivy League universities or the things that were destroyed to make them). For *our* family, though, configured the way we were, it was the perfect match for misery, Emersonian correspondence (there was an Emerson Circle as well) with a Kafkaesque spin to it—instead of wonder interlocking with wonder, the arrow finding its wound.

Olga and Zdenek. What could have been more perfectly designed to break them than life on Lord Byron Drive? There they were, after Italy and the Arafura Sea and the slums of Sydney, after Munich and New York, finally brought to ground. Surrounded by "Up with People" neighbors who could talk about Lehigh wrestling and lawn care and how awful it is what happens when the blacks move in but had no interest in politics or history, in Cambodia or Malcolm X or, for that matter, any of the writers their lanes and circles were named after. Who could mention Jesus and real estate values in the same sentence. Who'd say "My, but you two certainly do have a lot of books" but never, ever, go over to look at them. Who'd call you "my dear" (even though they were two years older), while explaining, patiently, "how things were" in America.

They laughed along for years, tried to fake it, tried to work up an opinion on the new restaurant opening at the Westgate Mall or whether Freedom High or Liberty would win the homecoming game, but it was no use. They were the exceptions to the American Dream, pieces of the mosaic that didn't quite fit and that the myth of integration couldn't acknowledge. Like so many others, they were the ones whose irony or range of references continually gave them away, whose attempts at humor fell flat, whose past pulled the conversation into contexts no one was interested in and few understood, whose Ghanian or Senegalese or Hindi-inflected English might pass at the office but would keep them from being invited to watch the game on Sunday because, you know, people just wanted to relax.

This was a different kind of exile, one with few solutions. While the majority of immigrants might eventually work their way in, often by outdoing the Americans in their "Americanness," for those like my parents, my mother especially, there were three options: live in a city diverse enough to make your otherness acceptable, surround yourself with émigrés like yourself—that is, live in an immigrant ghetto—or slip into a perpetual state of mourning for the deep, maternal familiarity of your language, the smells and tastes of home—that Eden you'd barely escaped.

New York had made the first two possible; our move to Bethlehem (and my mother's nature) made the third inevitable. Like a long-dormant seed, her talent for regret began to grow. Isolated for months, then years, driving the same two miles to the Westgate Mall or out to the south side past the abandoned steel mills looming over the Lehigh River, she reached some sort of tipping point. Hope, like anything else, has a half-life.

It was a hard thing to watch. I would have spared her if I could.

In *The Visible World* I let her step in front of a bus, leaving behind nothing more than a casserole dish half-filled with ashes and a few feathery bits of letter paper.

It should have been a hellish scene to write. It felt like a lungful of air.

In the dream-time of the novel, it was 1984. We were living in Bethlehem. Which seems right.

XLI

IT'S GETTING HARDER TO hold together. Like a character in a slapstick comedy trying to set up a tent (I vaguely recall Rock Hudson doing just that somewhere), the pieces of this story seem increasingly misaligned; when I insert one, another comes loose, demands attention. I need to pause, reset.

I need to acknowledge that you don't imagine your mother's death, even in a novel, without there maybe, just maybe, being some issues to think about.

I need to talk about betrayal. And guilt, its Siamese twin. And rage, their problematic offspring.

It begins with my mother's father, František Kubík. His was the original sin, the featuring blow, and like all acts of abuse—even those far less horrific—it was a betrayal of trust. At some point—when, exactly, I'll never know—that awful line was crossed, then crossed again. It's not news that people do unspeakable things to each other—even, at times, to those they should be closest to.

It doesn't take long for a cancer like that, left unacknowledged, to metastasize, and because it's in your heart, your mind, the turning cells, so to speak, are everywhere. Outside of you, the world mimics your betrayal—the smallest leaf puts out its shape. And how could it not? You've been betrayed at the very root, at the very source of trust—how could your world not answer in kind?

Inside you, it's worse. Betrayal, at least, still places the crime where it belongs—outside of you; guilt brings it home and lays it at your door. It's your fault now. For having instigated it—because you must have, somehow. For having continued with it. For having been kicked out of your home when your guilt was discovered, exiled into marriage.

You'll tell no one, ever. Not your friends, not your lover, not your husband, not even your son—though there, strangely, you'll come close, tapping on that closed door, signaling something he can't imagine and you yourself barely believe anymore. When your mother dies, it will stagger you like no natural parting ever could: besides your father, she was the last one on earth who knew, and now she's gone. It doesn't matter. You'll bury this thing, you say to yourself (even as it shovels the dirt up around your throat).

And because it's easier than hating him—he's still your daddy, after all—you'll hate yourself. You're closer. Your face is always there in the mirror, your body ready to hurt. It's so convenient. After a few years you'll forget the source—hating yourself will feel like instinct.

But hate is late-stage, and it won't stop with you. It will spread, branch, interlace with the betraying world that grows all around you. Which is the cause and which the effect—whether the world betrays you first or your hate forces it to—is up for discussion. Extra credit.

Which is where I come in, making my entrance with my usual flair in a gush of blood and amniotic fluid—ready to play my role. Our case—yours and mine, Mom—will be different: no primal sin, no originating horror. We'll be echoes.

I'll love you, trust you—utterly. And you'll manage to hold on to that for a while. And then the pattern will assert itself. You'll be cruel, then hate me for it because, as you know so well, we hate the ones we're cruel to. You'll make me the responsible one. Though I'll bleed every time I touch you, though you'll be the one who leaves, I'll be the one hurting *you*. I'll become what I was always going to be—the betrayer.

And neatly closing the circle, I'll learn to hate you for it. For having betrayed my trust. For hating me. And then, because it's easier than hating you—but this landscape looks familiar, no?— I'll begin to hate myself. I must have done *something*. I'll fly to guilt like an arrow to its wound.

Until, gulping for air like a goldfish on the carpet, I'll put you in a book, then under a bus.

Until I make you a dog with razor blades for fur.

Only then will the merry-go-round begin to stutter, then stall.

XLII

IN THE COURTYARD BELOW the window Jan Masaryk jumped from (remembering to close it behind him), the Czechs erected a plaque. It took them a while to get the funding—those who'd helped Masaryk out the window had to clear the stage first.

The plaque gives the name and the relevant dates, then adds the motto of the Czech nation: *Pravda vítězí!* Truth prevails!

Which would normally be that—another boring plaque for schoolchildren to yawn over—except that this is Prague and the Czechs, whatever their faults, tend to apply reason to pap. Even if the pap happens to be their national motto.

An adjustment is necessary. The committee votes, the stone-carver is notified. And the plaque goes up in the courtyard: *Pravda vítězí . . . ale dá to fušku.* Truth prevails! . . . but it takes some sweat.

XLIII

AND SO, BACK IN good old Bethlehem, "Christmas City, U.S.A.," it all went sideways—slowly at first, then not so slowly. My father, as he had in 1945, the year he and my mother were married, buried himself in work, then added booze and the new hobby of running vast distances around the cornfields and subdivisions before having a smoke. My mother descended, methodically, rung by rung (though she'd regularly reverse direction for a day or a week) into depression punctuated by rages that would turn her features into a kind of broken mask—the face of someone who's just seen their family killed and is looking at the person responsible. More and more often, that person was me.

It's a feeling I'd only wish on my worst enemy.

The endless silence of those sleety December afternoons, the darkness setting in by four. There's no one to laugh with, no one to talk to—eventually your friends on TV have to go.

I didn't know she was going mad. Such an old-fashioned expression—"He's mad, I tell you!" At the time, unbelievably, it all seemed normal. At the time—but this is how it always works—

it was just Mom. Mom was sad. Mom was angry. When Mom flew into a screaming rage over nothing, over air, then locked herself in her bedroom for four days, emerging only at night to stagger down the hallway to the kitchen, her hands out to the walls as if walking the deck of a rolling ship (turning her face away if you happened to be coming out of the bathroom), I thought it was normal.

It didn't happen overnight. She struggled for a while. For a year she lived back in Tarrytown, New York, renting a room so she could finish up her years of service in her old job and earn her retirement, returning home for the weekends. I'd clean the house, buy flowers. I did what I could. I was a good-enough kid. If I'd been listening, I would have heard the whine of an incoming shell, and run.

By the time I was seventeen, and for years after whenever I'd come home, I'd wake up in the mornings and just lie in my bed, taking the pulse of the house. I could tell from the way a door clicked in its latch how bad it was; I could tell by the weight of the silence. Often it was less subtle. I'd pick up that horrible telltale hissing—my mother raging at my father yet still, absurdly, trying to keep her voice down, then a scream of rage and something smashing, then a second, two, and a door slamming so hard the water in my aquarium would tremble—and just stay in my room to shorten the time I'd have to spend outside of it.

I'm not making any claim to anything—this isn't *Queen for a Day*. I have no interest in hustling our unhappiness for a bit of misery cred and a shot at *Oprah*. What I'm interested in is at once more selfish and less sellable. I want to know what the fuck happened to us, and why, and why I couldn't see it. I want to know why I couldn't save us, though what I *really* want, I think, is absolution, the beginning of this sentence with the word "why" removed like a long thorn: *I want to know I couldn't save us.*

I had enough to do saving myself. On the afternoon of January 15, 1975, when I was almost seventeen, with my mother off in Tarry-town for the week and my father at work, I found myself wandering around the house, room to room, then down the hallway, then again. Aimlessly, pointlessly. Unable to work, to read, to sleep. Unable to stop. It was sleeting outside, and as I passed by the rooms, the windows looked like empty slides in a projector. The world seemed drained. I'd never known such loneliness. I didn't know what was happening to me. I felt like I couldn't breathe.

"Life was a death sentence," my mother said.

I couldn't stop walking—it was a small house—back and forth, back and forth. I'd promise myself that on the next go-round I'd stop, and then the next—and then I'd walk right through, berating myself for my weakness. I thought I was going crazy. I remember trying to laugh, then getting down on the floor and knocking out a bunch of push-ups, then scaring myself by starting to cry.

I took a blank notebook off the shelf, scrawled the date— January 15, 1975—on the first page with a Bic pen and began describing the sea I was drowning in.

I've never stopped.

XLIV

I DIDN'T SEE THE PILLS. I didn't even imagine them. And now that I know about them, all they do is confuse things. I'd like to Google it: "*What percentage of mom was the Lexaurin singing in her skull?*" then press RETURN.

We had a pact, Mom and I: We would always tell each other the truth. Always. No matter what. From the time I was old enough to understand, this was the rock of our church: Her word or mine, once asked for and given, was the one thing we could depend on in this life. If that trust was ever broken between us, she'd tell me, the tears welling up in her eyes, she might as well kill herself.

I believed her.

As far back as I can remember, there's my mother, warning me about the perils of addiction. Addiction terrified and disgusted her. Addictive personalities—like my father's—were weak; they gave in, they bent under their personal unhappiness. They lacked that certain something, that inner core; they broke. You had to feel sorry for these people—it wasn't their fault—but so it was. Some just had it—*it* being associated by now with having a limit, throwing the peach, being a man, breaking down the door—others didn't.

Mom, of course, had it. Not that she didn't understand, you understand—the temptation could be great—but alcohol, or "drugs," or even sleeping pills, given a chance, would make you their slave. You had to keep them in their place through sheer force of will. And to show me what she meant, to demonstrate the indomitable power of *her* will, she'd take me by the hand and lead me to her dresser and show me the pills she kept hidden in her drawer. There they were. She'd taken one once, she'd say, pointing—it had been prescribed to her by her doctor—and it had been wonderful; she'd slept like a child, woken happy, floated through her day. . . . She still remembered it, and for *precisely* that reason she'd never take one again; more, to dominate the temptation, the memory of that treacherous peace, she'd keep them close. Just to prove her own strength. Now and then she'd take them out and look at them—then put them back in their place.

In the spring of 2003 my father and I were having a drink in our café in the same inner mall on Vinohradská Street we always went to, when the subject of Mom came up. He and I didn't talk about her much, but she was always there. At that point I hadn't spoken to her for seven years.

What happened to us? I asked him that afternoon, pretty much out of the blue.

He glanced at me with those slightly watery eyes—part drink, part age, part love.

It was just that I'd never really understood what went wrong, I said—why she hated me. Why she seemed to need to think the worst of me—or him, for that matter; to treasure every word I'd ever said to her in anger—or, if necessary, make up my sins from scratch. Where did it all come from—the crazy rages, the business of locking herself away for days over nothing, of thinking me evil for packing a t-shirt?

I remember him tilting his head in that way he had whenever the question was bigger than the answer, then looking at the fake plants by the bar. He had his shot of vodka by him, his seltzer water, his cigarettes. They'd been divorced for a decade by now; he'd remarried years ago—a decent, unvarying, sane woman.

"You have to remember, your mother had a lot to carry," he said vaguely. "It wasn't about you."

He paused.

"Well, obviously it *was* about you—involved you. And I'm sorry for that." He shook his head. "This is hard for you to see, but she loved you."

"I know she did," I said. "Once."

"In many ways she was a lot like her own father," he said, thinking aloud. "So full of anger. And then of course there were the pills. . . ."

"What pills?" I said.

He looked at me. "Your mother was addicted to pills for almost thirty years," he said. "Still is, probably. Surely you knew that."

I didn't say anything.

"I tried to get her to get help, to come to AA with me."

"Pills?" I said.

"She'd never admit she had a problem. Our good friend Slavka—remember her?—kept her supplied for years; your mother would call her whenever she was running low, then meet her in the city." He lit a cigarette with those wide, worker's hands, took a drag. "It's important to have friends in this world, don't you think?"

I heard what he said, and I didn't. It was as if my mind simply set it aside—"I'll deal with this later." I was forty-five years old, with a family of my own, yet part of me still accepted the story I'd been told as a priori truth: My father was the addictive personality, not my mother. My mother was the one standing before the dresser drawer, pointing out the things that would make her weak. She'd never give in. She'd never lie to me.

On a cool and cloudless July morning in 2014, a day after visiting my mother in the care home in Brno, my wife and daughter and I made our way to Zadní Vydří, the tiny medieval village where my mother had lived the last twenty years of her life with a man named Mr. Černý. Getting there wasn't easy. Flummoxed by detours and road signs that seemed to lead us in circles (in 1968 the Czechs had delayed the Soviet tanks for two days by rearranging the road signs, a gesture at once grimly amusing, ultimately pointless and very Czech), we bumped through slate-roofed towns essentially unchanged for centuries, down miles of tree-lined country roads flashing with sun and shadow, and eventually found our way to my mother's stuccoed little "villa" more or less by accident. We bumped to a stop, got out of the car. Two clouded carp ponds, the sudden silence of the fields. We hadn't been there in years. It didn't look as if anybody had.

The twenty-foot dirt driveway was knee-high in grass, the gate in the wall rusted shut, the courtyard a waist-high jungle of nettles and weeds. Under the apple trees, wasps buzzed on the rotting fruit. Our daughter tried one key, then another, then a third.

When we shoved open the door, a cold, mildewed rush of air pushed past as if escaping into the sun, and then we just stood there, feeling like we'd burst in on something shameful, humiliating.

This was like entering a troubled mind: black mold grew in the corners by the ceiling, the ripped arms of the recliner were wet to the touch. Stuffed into corners or piled haphazardly on the damp carpet were bags of dead batteries, twenty-three broken watches (we counted), fifteen pairs of eyeglasses, used hypodermic needles and bloody cotton swabs in jars (Černý had been a diabetic). Stacked high along the walls were moldering books and piles of *Prevention* magazine from the mid 1970s; in the peeling TV console, next to warped LPs by Karel Gott and Andy Williams, dozens of used adult diapers. The old beige sofa we used to sit on in Bethlehem was there, and the slice-of-a-tree coffee table, and a flat, faded mat that looked like our cat, Chiquita's, old, embroidered cushion.

In the bedroom the French doors to the courtyard had been boarded up and nailed shut. With a flashlight that we found in the kitchen, I picked my way through the dark piles of cracking suitcases and picture frames and broken exercise equipment hung with the dresses and pants suits I could remember my mother wearing to her job at Pocantico Hills where I used to run off into the woods.

A path, narrow as a deer trail, ran from the door to the bed. On the night table was a photograph of her holding me as a baby on Jones Beach, another of F. as a young man, squinting into the sun, and a spoon.

I'd written to her here, argued and pleaded with her on the phone while she sat on this bed, tried to talk her into leaving. Nothing would move her. She was barricaded in, screaming for help.

Once she'd called me in the winter, when we were living on the Canadian border—it was almost two in the morning, her time. Crying, incoherent, raging at her companion—Černý. I tried to say something, comfort her. He was hiding her documents from her, the bastard, controlling her every move. I could hear him yelling back, an old man pushed to the limit, playing for keeps.

And then she forgot I was there. They both did. I could hear them screaming, now closer, now farther off. There'd be a lull—during which I'd yell into the phone, hoping she'd hear me—and then the fight would explode again. I stayed on the line for almost an hour, then hung up. When I called back, the phone was busy. It stayed busy.

I called my father, who called the town's mayor, who put on his boots and crossed the grassy walk between the carp ponds at dawn and banged on the gate. My mother was fine, he said.

The pills were in an empty food carton in a broken wardrobe in the main room—hundreds of empty, cellophane-backed pill packets, maybe a dozen or two still unused. The carton ripped wetly when I pulled it out and small, black bugs scattered into a pile of 8-track tapes. The names of the pills meant nothing to me.

That night in our hotel in Brno our daughter looked them up on the Internet and the answer came back from the ether.

This is what I learned: That my mother had been an addict for many years. That benzodiazepines, the class of drugs she'd been addicted to, were developed in the 1970s for the short term relief of severe anxiety and insomnia. That they were so highly addictive the FDA was attempting to have them reclassified as Class A drugs, like heroin. That trying to get off them could stop your heart. That our good friend Slavka, who'd supplied her, was essentially a criminal with an M.D.

It wasn't enough. Or too much—the one-word answer to every question. Scrolling down through the side effects was like watching an old home movie, now with added narration: "Look, look—see there? That's your mother's free-floating 'anxiety,' the 'changes of perception and feelings of unreality,' and here—see how she's staggering down the hallway at night?—that's the typical 'loss of balance,' and here—where she's coming apart on the way out of Rotterdam?—that's the 'panic attacks' and the 'paranoia,' the 'persistent and unpleasant memories' and the 'short-term memory loss.' Oh, and here, where she's sitting by the shore of Skalák in her tight-around-the-ankle slacks counting out the number of pills needed to kill her, there you have the 'suicidal thoughts'—

always an ironic side effect of any 'medication'—and finally—
we're almost done—here we are in the care home in Brno, the
gift bag at the end of the party—the *heightened risk of dementia
and Alzheimer's.*'"

It was something. It wasn't enough. Though they explained
some things—allowed me to draw a line between the causes in
column A and the effects in column B—the pills weren't enough.

They were the accelerant, not the match.

XLV

I THINK IT'S FAIR to say that sex was always a problem for my mother. A kind of haunted haven.

She was Gretel, wandering out of the forest where bad things had happened, only now the story had changed: In this version she was dropping bread crumbs so she could find her way back. She didn't want to drop them. She couldn't stop herself. Each one tied her to the thing she'd escaped from.

Looking back, I see that some of the bread crumbs were more telling than others, but they were always about fear.

Homophobia was a theme. When I was in third grade, for example, she worried a good deal about my friend Kevin. Had I noticed anything strange about him? Some boys had certain "tendencies"—she didn't expect me to understand. It was just that she'd seen us wrestling in the yard and, well, his head had ended up in a place it shouldn't have ended up; anyway, now that she thought about it, she'd prefer I play with the other boys. And because I didn't have a clue what she was talking about and didn't really care about Kevin one way or the other except for the fact that he'd let me win when we flipped for baseball cards, I did what Mommy said.

Kevins were everywhere, apparently. My college roommate was a possible Kevin, what with that gold chain he wore around his neck—this or that acquaintance showed unmistakable signs. My father's Kevin-ness, of course, came up as predictably as crocuses in spring: just as Dad was literally color-blind, he was blind the other way—*you* know. Gina Lollobrigida could walk in front of him stark naked and he'd never see a thing.

Nor were Kevins restricted to the, ahem, male gender: a certain salesgirl at Macy's, helping her try on a blouse, had touched her inappropriately; a notorious lesbian at Teachers College at Columbia (where my mother received her librarian's degree) had "cornered her" in the stacks. And so on.

If it's easy for me to make light of now (my mother escaped the stacks unscathed), it's because condescension masks complicity. For a long time I bought this "deviance" narrative (as common in the general culture then as the notion of, say, black inferiority twenty years earlier), just like I did all the others she told me, because there was profit in it—Daddy's less-than-manliness, which she described to me in detail, reflected well on me. By the time I appeared in the crosshairs and my own sexuality became a cause for concern (did I have other friends besides my roommate?), a lot of opportunities for doing the right thing had passed me by. It's one of my regrets, and if it's true that mine were only sins of omission (I didn't care enough to argue with my roommate's typical—and, under the circumstances, deeply ironic—Jamaican homophobia), they're no more excusable for that.

But if the Kevins were a problem, the Amys and Maries of the world were, too. More, because I obviously cared for them. Because they'd take me away. Because I'd go willingly, betray her. Because it was an inescapable fact that (insert the Czech version here) "your daughter's your daughter the rest of your life; your son is your son till he takes a wife," and as it was written (somewhere) so it must be. Betrayal was obligatory.

That I wasn't thinking of matrimony that summer at Twin Lakes when I was twelve didn't really matter—it had begun. The process that would leave her alone, broken, forgotten. She wouldn't let me go easily.

I didn't realize this. I was too busy listening to Bread's "I Want to Make It with You" on the radio. I was standing under the paper lanterns, frozen like a frog in the flashlight's beam by my first actual glimpse of a "woman's" breasts. I was lying out on the float dreaming of ways to impress her (this girl with breasts)— imagining what I might say to her if she ever actually noticed me, what she'd do if I ever found the courage to take her hand.

The rainy August day in 1970 that I bicycled over to the deserted "campus" from our house to hang out with Karen, her brother, Kevin (a different one), and their stepsister, Laura, I had no idea what I was getting into.

The afternoon passed quickly, I remember, with the clouds flying low over the late-summer fields and the rain pattering on the tin roof of the rec house where we played game after game of Ping-Pong, no doubt yelling and insulting each other the way twelve-year-olds always have and will. I have a vague memory of showing off, tirelessly—giddy as a colt in clover at finding myself in the company of not one, but two pretty girls, one of whom I liked, and the other who liked me. I have no idea what we talked about and it doesn't matter. All I recall—and this I recall so vividly—was an odd and oddly unforgettable thing that occurred later in the after-noon during a pause in the rain.

We'd been hanging about in a half-mowed field by the mess hall when a field mouse bolted out of the grass, realized its error, then pinballed between us like a cartoon. I grabbed it—because that's what I do, grab things—and being a manly sort of mouse it promptly sank its little yellow incisors into my thumb, earning itself a quick trip, airmail, back to its home.

I was ripe for humiliation, just sitting on the trip-wire chair like in the old carnivals, ready to be dunked by the first good shot. What could possibly be less cool than grabbing a mouse, getting bit, and actually yelling out with surprise and pain? To my amaze-ment, nobody took me down. Kevin held his tongue, the girls made a fuss over me: I was bleeding—wounded. Out of nowhere, Laura produced a tube of antibiotic cream and a box of Band-Aids. Sitting opposite me on the wet grass, she took my hand in hers—I was sure she could hear my heart pounding like a tom-tom in my chest—cleaned off the bite, then slowly, tenderly (with Karen leaning over to offer advice), made me whole.

It was only then that I noticed the time: I was almost an hour late already. Still dazed—more in love than I'd been before, though with whom I wasn't quite sure anymore—I jumped on my bike and flew the five miles back to the turnoff to our house by the lake. Would that I'd kept going, joined the circus.

My father wasn't home. My mother was. I barely recognized her.

I was late—why was I late?

I was sorry, I stammered, I'd forgot, I didn't mean—

"Co je s tebou?—What's the matter with you? Why are you so flushed?"

"I'm not, I just—"

"Why do you have that look?"

"What look? I don't—"

"What happened?"

"Nothing happened," I said, raising my voice, because something *had* happened, a girl had held my hand, "I don't know what you're talking about, nothing happened—"

"Who do you think you are, taking that tone?"

"I'm not . . . I don't—"

"Listen to yourself—why are you overreacting like this? Tell me what happened! What happened with those girls? Were you alone? Tell me!"

I don't remember if she smacked me, but if she had, it would have been a relief. It went on. It was the first of its kind and it came out of nowhere, a vicious, crying fight—me doing the crying, of course, humiliated, guilty over thoughts I'd been harboring for weeks (but how could she know?), old enough to understand what she was implying, too young to not be ashamed of having imagined it.

There'd be a long line of Karens. When Linda, to whom I'd declared my love the third week of my freshman year at Ardsley High School, came to our house with a friend of hers—a kind of designated speaker who managed to squeeze out, "Hi, Mrs. Slouka, can Mark come out to play?"—both girls were sent packing in no uncertain terms. When Denise, who I dated in college, surprised me by catching a bus to Bethlehem one evening on a whim (bringing flowers for my mother), she was told she was not welcome in our house and could make her own arrangements for a place to sleep. When I wanted to visit Amy in California, who I missed desperately, funds were withdrawn and roadblocks erected. When Marie, a girl I'd fallen in love with as a twenty-one-year-old in Czechoslovakia, left a message with my mother asking if I'd meet her at the Brno train station to say goodbye (I'd written, after weeks of arguments at home, to break off our relationship), I wasn't given the message, nor told that she'd waited for me that afternoon until many years later when a friend of my mother's told me the truth.

Looking back, I see it as a kind of tug-of-war, with my mother on one side and the handful of girls I'd known and cared for on the other, pulling me, through kindness, decency and just-plain-normalness toward the man I'd become—the man, ironically, my mother had once intended me to be. That they squeaked out a victory still fills me with gratitude.

It wasn't easy. Or pretty. The tug-of-war would go on for years. As I began pulling away from her (she'd make sure of it), my mother found herself fighting a war of attrition against any and all, deploying troops in direct proportion to how much I actually seemed to care for the girl in question, resorting to propaganda, risking everything until, at long last, reality outran apprehension and I met the woman I'd marry. By this point, almost Lear-like, she was striking around herself with anything that came to hand, even at one point summoning up a grotesque and flatly unbelievable anti-Semitism as if that might somehow carry the day. I fought her to a bloody standstill (neither of us inclined to give by this point), then realized that the person I was marrying—vestigially Jewish, utterly kind—was invisible to her. She was flailing at ghosts—reason had little to do with it.

And what ghosts they were—whispering, suggesting, drawing vague connections between memory and nightmare, then pulling them tight. . . . All the years I knew her, for example, whenever she needed to pull a sweater over her head, she'd first carefully gather it up in a thick necklace, then tear it over her face like something on fire. There had been that time, she'd say, when she was still just a little girl, when "a stranger" had trapped her in her own dress. Since then, she couldn't stand the feeling of being closed in. And so the blouses and sweaters and sweatshirts came off the way they did.

And then the sweater got caught on a necklace, or an earring, or just slipped out of her hands. The panic—wild, flailing, drowning panic—was instant. A lamp smashed, an earring tore. My father, leaping to help, took an elbow in the face.

Which was bad enough. What terrified me then—what terrifies me still—was the sound she made, trapped inside that sweater. She wasn't screaming; she was whimpering.

———————

At the last minute, forced into it by my father, she came to our wedding. A wonderfully still, sun-filled, early-October morning. I have a photograph of her sitting next to Leslie at lunch after the ceremony that day in Charlottesville. She talked to the bride about death for two hours—not the usual topic for wedding lunches—and the photographs bear it out. The Czechs have an expression for it—*strhanej obličej*—a face like something torn down. The look of a world ending, of bottomless despair.

It was only recently, while going through the mildewed suitcase of old pictures we brought back from her house in Vydří, that I recognized that wedding-day look—a look of grief bordering on terror—on another photograph: It shows my mother, supported by my great-uncle Pepa, walking in to her father's funeral.

XLVI

THERE ARE THINGS YOU bury, things you wall up. Because you have to. It's not a choice.

Neither is unearthing them when the time comes.

I remember the rainy afternoon my mother and I spent sitting in the median of the highway outside of Rotterdam as one of the most surreal of my life. It didn't get better. She was bottoming quickly, rocked by storms I couldn't see, turning on me in ways I hadn't known before, with a kind of out-of-body ferocity, then slipping into a state of weeping depression bordering on catatonia. I fought back when I had to, tried to comfort her when she turned the guns on herself. Neither made the slightest difference.

I can't convey the helplessness of those days any more than I already have: the hours of silence, my mother driving with the tears rolling out from under her Jackie O. sunglasses, her face twitching and flinching to some inner dialogue as I try to hide inside my 1980-era headphones (plugged into a little tape-player by my feet), listening to America's "Horse with No Name" and imagining myself with my friend Geoff in the High Sierra. Trying not to notice that the tears have stopped, ominously, trying not to feel her rage gathering but seeing it everywhere, in the bunched-up lines of her mouth, in the more relaxed, ready-for-battle slope of her shoulders, knowing it's coming. . . . *The ocean is a desert with its life underground.* . . .

I can't tell you if it was that night or the next. I can't tell you where it was—somewhere in Germany, I think. I just remember my mother, though barely able to speak by now, getting the room. A small hotel by the side of the road. Darkness outside. Wooden floors.

There was one bed, possibly queen-size, maybe larger. And because my mind desperately wants to be elsewhere, I suddenly see Steve Martin and John Candy in *Planes, Trains and Automobiles* walking into the motel room they're forced to share for the night and panicking when they see there's only one bed.

I don't know if I offered to sleep on the floor, if it even occurred to me. I don't remember if we ate something. All I remember is getting to the room and my mother being terribly disturbed by the bed, raging at the hotel people, then me—muttering something about how this explained things, why I hated her—and me not knowing what the hell she was talking about. After the days in Rotterdam, the craziness in the port, the madness in the median, the endless fights, I was completely drained—wanting only to sleep till September when I could be done with this fucking insanity and go back to school. There was plenty of room, I said.

My mother wasn't talking anymore. She was staggering with exhaustion, forcing this fake-sounding cough she always deployed when overwhelmed, attacked, betrayed by the world. Asking—*hack, hack*—for sympathy—she was ill, couldn't you see?—even as she cut you.

She'd taken some *prášky*, she said, coughing. Some pills. She got stranger, mumbling to herself as if I wasn't there, then looking at me like she couldn't believe I was her son. She didn't know what had happened to me—how I'd come to be so full of hate. Become such a liar. She had to sleep. It didn't matter. Nothing mattered.

I fell into bed, sank deep, then woke into the near dark. It felt late. I was lying on my side, facing away from my mother. The bed was trembling in a way I thought at first was her crying, but wasn't. Then I heard her breathing and understood what I was hearing and after that I didn't hear any more. It went on a long time. I didn't move. I lay there, frozen, until it was over and then for a long time after that and then I fell asleep.

I didn't mention it to a soul. I didn't write about it in my journal. Some things you just wall up. They don't exist.

That night didn't exist for thirty-five years, until the summer of 2014 when I saw my mother in the care home, then went through the devastation of her villa in Vydří. In some way those two things together—seeing her, then seeing the place she'd lived in—kicked a window in the wall, forced me to see things I didn't want to see. Drowned kittens in a pail. That night in Germany.

I've tried to convince myself it didn't happen. Because I don't want this memory of my poor mother who, at that moment, in her insanity, probably didn't even know I was there. Because I don't want this picture of myself, helpless, terrified at the age of twenty-two.

Now that it's mine, I'd like to core it out of my brain like a tumor. I can't. Acknowledging it is as close as I'll come. It'll have to do.

XLVII

IN ONE OF MY favorite Kafka parables, a powerful messenger is summoned by the emperor and given a message to deliver. He starts off immediately, "thrusting out one hand, then the other," pointing to the imperial star on his breast, but though the crowd parts before him, obstacles flower, the way thickens with history and men. It will take him years to make his way through the inner courtyards, and beyond these are others, vaster, more crowded, and beyond them others still . . . it will never be. The imperial message, meant expressly for you, can never arrive.

I always believed the imperial message answered the riddle of the self; that breaking open the seal, you'd know who you are.

Then again, what would be the fun of that? And why would you believe it? Better to cobble the answer yourself, take your enlightenment as it comes.

Sometimes enlightenment can arrive in humble packages, plainly wrapped. I was thinking about where fate or foolishness had brought me a few winters back—it's a kind of hobby with me—when a line from a third-rate John Fogerty song forced a small recognition: *It took years of effort, to become the mess that you see.* I was rowing nowhere at the time, sitting on a machine in a freezing, glassed-in porch in a rented house on the Canadian border. The machine had a handle attached to a chain, a sliding seat, and a small screen which kept track of precisely how far I hadn't, in fact, gone, and how many calories I'd burned not getting there. I was dressed in thermals and a winter hat. In my mind, I was outrowing Newt Gingrich and the president of a small liberal arts college in Annandale-on-Hudson who I believed to be a pompous ass. It seemed normal.

It was then that Fogerty, forty years past his Creedence Clearwater days but still playing the "rambunctious boy," knocked on my door. *It took years of effort. . . .* Yes, well. *Whose effort* was the question.

Dusk, the sky like a bell, heat rushing up from the earth. An introspective season. The snow on the roofs in the last light looked blue; a single window shone from the house across the way. At twenty below, my students had told me, soap bubbles crystallize and quietly shatter.

My father died before the next snow.

Short of an imperial message, I wonder what can explain us? The way we are with the world, the bickering parts? Is it all just Mummy and Daddy, forever shouting up the double helix to our room? Is it something chemical, ironic by virtue of its smallness—

too much garlic down the umbilical cord? Did some pudgy-legged deity, pulling apart the primordial Play-Doh, pause in mid-mitosis, and laugh? And lay us aside?

Forced to call it, I'd go with a combination of acts and accidents: things done, words withheld, and sheer dumb luck.

Beyond that, I have no idea. Some things stick to us, others don't. Some of the things we do we learn to recognize and avoid; others—the vast majority—are invisible to us. We're a mass of effects cut off from their causes, a crime scene with a million clues. Good luck playing detective. *It took years of effort* . . .

Blaming Mom and Dad for the "mess that you see" is traditional but there's not much profit in it and what little there is devalues with age. Better, I think, to put together a list of "Acknowledgments"— the kind you'd find in the back of a book written by someone with too many friends—or given to currying favor.

Finally, I'd like to thank my parents, Zdenek and Olga Slouka:

For my overdeveloped nose for beauty and regret, my capacity for pain, my compensatory sense of humor.

For my dreams, which are ungodly; for my love of music and words.

For the natural world, which has been my haven—from them and everything else.

For the way I overreact to perceived unfairness—something a long line of "superiors" have come to know well. For my awkwardness with praise; for my trademark blend of insecurity and confidence.

For my loyalty. For my readiness to walk the fuck out.

For my positively statesmanlike reasonableness—and my willingness to throw the peach.

For my distrust of surfaces.

For my obsession with justice, which I hunger for the way some men lust for God.

For the way I incline toward the past (and the present), toward solitude (and the company of friends), toward silence (and laughter).

For the way I'm always mourning the last place I left.

For the fact that the easiest way to piss me off is not to tell me what's pissing you off because it drops me, even at the age of fifty-seven, straight down the "What did I do, Mommy?" rabbit hole, which in turn makes me so furious that I overcompensate by blowing up the rabbit hole.

For my oversensitivity to rudeness and my proportionally excessive gratitude for the smallest civility, kindness, or act of generosity.

For my pitch-perfect ear for mortality, which saturates my world with fear and wonder.

For my persistence. Tenacity. Fine—stubbornness.

And my problem(s) with authority. And bullies of all sizes and stripes. For my instinct to charge the thing that frightens me.

For my vaguely Old World (and very expensive) disdain for self-promotion; for my utter inability to network; for my dog-like devotion to talent (as defined by me, of course) wherever it appears.

For my sentimentality, which I keep on a leash though it regularly chews free, digs under the fence, gives me away.

For all the fistfights I had as a kid, which I never sought but which seemed to find *me*; for the snot and blood on my collar.

But this last item might be worth a carrot in the manuscript.

Once upon a time, when I was fourteen, I was walking around a reedy mountain lake in the High Sierra when I came across a young man squashing frogs with a flat rock. I was no hero, semi-tough at best, and this kid had a couple of years and thirty pounds on me. I told him to knock it off and he told me to go fuck myself. When I was safely out of reach, I yelled back—my voice shaking, probably, because by now I knew where this was going—that if I found him doing it again I'd kick his ass, and he laughed.

I happen to like frogs; the gold dust in a frog's eye is one of the most beautiful things in the world.

I spent the next twenty minutes working myself into a froth, then came around to find him doing what he'd been doing before. He'd pick up the rock, wait patiently till a frog surfaced, then drop it. So I snuck up and punted him into the pond—a big, uninhibited, Ode-to-Joy-ish kick in the ass (and whatever was adjacent to it, most likely, because he spent a long time on his hands and knees in the shallows). He didn't come after me. By now I had a rock in one hand and a good stick in the other. If I'd had a boulder, he'd have ended up like Piggy in *Lord of the Flies*. Eventually I left.

Flying out over the water, his back humped up and his legs trailing, he'd looked oddly like a leaping frog. Which made me happy.

He deserved it. I've never been able to tolerate cruelty—

another thing I'd like to thank my mother for. Still, my blood-in-the-eye willingness to brain him with a rock that day may have had other roots.

That was the summer I learned we were moving to Bethlehem because Dad was an alcoholic and Mom couldn't risk him "driving those distances"; the summer I was told we'd had to give up our cabin at Lost Lake and wouldn't be going back; the summer my mother took me out for boysenberry pie at the Grants Grove Lodge and told me about F.——a man she'd known and cared for many years ago and still thought about sometimes.

I reminded her of him, she said. I had his walk.

XLVIII

MID-MAY, 2015. I'M BACK at Lost Lake. I've been writing here
for some weeks now, watching the season come on, gradually losing the thermals, the ski hat, the fingerless gloves. Shedding like a
snake. The stone wall is where I left it last fall, angling down into
the water. A pair of phoebes have built their annual nest under the
eave. I check it daily with a long-handled mirror as part of my
prewriting ritual: two white eggs the size of jelly beans.

It's occurred to me lately that my mother might die while I
write this book. That she's linked to it. That somehow, 6,000 miles
away, though she hasn't moved or spoken in months, she's aware
of it.

I should write her story, she used to tell me. I'd rather have
stuck needles in my eyes.

It wasn't mine to tell, I'd say—it was hers. Or I'd kick it
down the road to never: "Who knows?" I'd tell her. "Maybe I
will, someday."

Well, never's here. It's mine to tell now. I like to think she'd
approve of the telling, but I don't know.

I know it's crazy, this link I've made between her life and these pages—mystical bullshit if ever there was any—and yet I can't shake it. I feel like she's waiting for me to finish.

The stones of the wall past the window screen. The Adirondack chairs in the shade of the oaks, too rickety to sit in. When the breeze picks up, I can hear the rainy sound of the wind in the leaves. This doubled shoreline, this small, dark lake—are haunted by us.

And I can't write fast enough.

XLVIX

SOMETIME IN THE FALL of 1944, egged on by her friend Jiřinka, my mother had her fortune told to her by an arthritic crone in a colorful shawl not far from the Brno train station. A small, dark apartment smelling of cats, low lamp light, the unavoidable beads. The Gypsy woman, who my mother said had disconcertingly light-gray eyes, like an old dog's, sat down opposite her on a small stool, took her hand, stroked it with the backs of her fingers, then glanced down at the open palm and froze. Eventually, she spoke. She was sorry, she said, but the lines didn't lie. My mother would leave her home country. She'd live in a foreign land for many years. She'd marry, have one child—a son. But she'd return home alone, having lost us both. She was sorry—there was no mistake. And she offered to waive her fee.

For twenty-five years my mother lived in fear of that fortune, ridiculing herself for her superstition yet terrified that something— a moment's inattention on the highway—would make the prophesy true.

The Gypsy was wrong. And not.

In 1969, my parents returned to Czechoslovakia—a quick, two-day, heart-in-your-throat kind of strike across the border that must have seemed completely unreal to them both. I was eleven years old.

How, exactly, it came to pass I don't know. This was a year after the Soviet invasion, a time of considerably heightened risk, and yet for some reason they'd been granted visas (had the charges against them been dropped?) and there we were, in a boxy blue rental car, approaching the border at Střehov. The unsmiling guards in their green uniforms with the red stripe on the visored cap thumbed through our American passports, then asked us to step out of the car. It took them two hours: every book was turned upside down and shaken, every piece of makeup scrutinized. When we finally got back in the car and the gates rose and we drove through toward the ruined castle looming over the road, something inside my mother was released. We were with her. The Gypsy had been wrong.

I've tried to imagine what it must have been like for them. I've tried to imagine myself living in China, say, for twenty-one years—unable to return home, unable to communicate, hearing of one parent's death, then the other's—all the time dreaming of walking through the sliding doors at Kennedy into a hot New York night with the cabs blaring and the luggage guys yelling to each other and some guy with an employee badge on his shirt saying to his buddy, "And I'm like, whadda you kiddin' me?" and then suddenly finding myself walking through those doors, smelling those smells, hearing that laughter—laughter that'd been there, incredibly, all the years I'd been away.

I've tried to imagine it. I don't think I came close. Not just because for them the intoxication of returning home was cut by fear—the regime hadn't changed, and the chance that "something might happen" was considerable—but because nothing could have prepared them for what they found: Nothing had changed.

It must have seemed, quite literally, unbelievable—a waking dream. In the normal run of things, after all, the world goes on after we leave, antiquing our recollections of it: neighborhoods decline or come up, people move, our best friend's home is an office building. It's a mercy disguised as heartache: Returning home, we're forced to reconcile the new world with the one we remembered, and it's this business of reconciliation that buffers our hearts, gentles our ascent.

There'd be no buffer for my parents. This was a memory come alive.

I remember the growing silence in the car, the speechlessness of amazement: There was that place, and that one, and, "Oh, my God, look!" Eventually we stopped before a nondescript seven-story apartment building in the Žabovřesky district of Brno. A warm, late-summer afternoon, the street already half in shade as if filling with water. My mother pointed up: her best friend Jiřinka had lived right there, she said, shaking her head. She remembered the building. She'd always wave up at her so she wouldn't have to walk up the stairs, and Jiřinka would come down and they'd go to the Přehrada or the movies.

We got out of the car. I was bored. It was a building.

It was like yesterday, my mother was saying—just like yesterday. Twenty-one years. She remembered which window was hers, six floors up—and she began to count—and seven over: one, two, three . . .

And then she didn't say anything more because Jiřinka, a middle-aged woman now, had swung the windows into the late sun and glanced out over the street as if still, after all those years, watching for her friend.

L

THE NEAR-MISS, THE ALMOST-ACCIDENT, is always a source of
wonder. Things went the way they did; two inches over, everything would have been different.

That first trip to Czechoslovakia was a near-miss for us, the closest we ever had as a family. We sneezed and the bullet ruffled
our hair. We bent to tie our shoes. Still, if the dice had rolled
differently that day, if my parents had been arrested as American
spies and sentenced to twenty years in the uranium mines (I'd
have been packed off to live with my maternal grandfather—an
interesting twist in the tale), it's fair to say there would have been
a certain humor in it.

As it happened, one or two things *had* changed.

It went like this. Heading for the border on the second day, my
father insisted on a detour: There was a certain place he'd known
as a boy—a view from a hill across a river valley. He'd been a

scout there, gone camping there as a young man, known a girl there. He wanted to see it.

Once on the track, typically, nothing would stop him. He found first this village, then that one, then a hardpack road sloping up through mustard and barley fields into the pines. Everything was coming back. We bumped and scraped along, the grain swishing against the sides of the car. A beautiful summer day, the shadows of small white clouds floating serenely across the fields. Everything was deserted.

My mother didn't like it. Something wasn't right. Why did all the fences have signs saying VSTUP ZAKÁZAN!—(Entrance Forbidden!)? she said.

What signs? my father said.

Signs. Like that one. And that one.

Those were for the cows, my father said, because he was my father. To keep them out of the fields, probably.

Nonsense, my mother said—cows didn't read, and the local farmers would know to keep them out of the fields. Plus there weren't any cows.

My father drove on. By God, he remembered this! It was just up this way.

Eventually we lurched to the top of a densely wooded hill and piled out of the car, my father, in his white tourist cap and black horn-rims, carrying his camera and lenses in a bag over his shoulder, my mother in her fashionable slacks and blouse, me in my humiliating German shorts and socks and sandals. The view should be just past those trees, my father said, heading off like an Indian scout.

At that point the sound of an approaching motor came through the trees and a man on a black motorcycle appeared on the road. He took in the Austrian plates on the car, our Western outfits, parked behind us and came over to chat. A man in his early forties, very polite. Years later I'd meet polite men like him in Nicaragua—men who'd conducted guerilla warfare in the jungle for six years.

A beautiful day, he said.

Yes, indeed, my father said. A magnificent day.

Every alarm bell in my mother's head was going off at once.

A beautiful day, the man said again, smiling. Could he help us find something, perhaps? He'd noticed we weren't from these parts.

No, no, my father said. It was very kind but he knew exactly where he was—there was a certain view, just over that way. . . .

A view?

A beautiful view, a river valley—he used to go camping there as a boy, such wonderful memories. He wanted to take some pictures.

I see, the man said. And—forgive me—you're Austrian?

American, actually.

American.

Born in Brno. Just here for a short visit.

The man took a pack of cigarettes out of his leather jacket, offered my father a cigarette, then took one for himself. A lovely camera—might he see it?

Of course.

The man looked through the viewfinder. Wonderful optics. He was guessing there was a telephoto lens in that beautiful bag.

Of course. And my father, happy to have made a friend, launched off on the virtues of various lenses while I started after some black and orange beetles I'd noticed on the forest floor and my mother stood there with both hands over her mouth, knowing we were plunging into something but still unsure of exactly how deep it was.

At some point the chatter was over, the smile gone. We needed to get back in the car, the man said, quietly. The view my father had been heading for with his American camera and his telephoto lens overlooked a protected military zone—surely we'd seen the signs?

My father blinked, still dense with sleep but waking quickly. Cows, he said. We thought they were for the cows.

No, the man said.

My mother would later claim that in that instant she saw something like pure amazement in his eyes.

One more thing, he said as we rushed to our car.

Yes?

Don't stop.

We didn't. I peed in a bottle, kneeling on the floor in the back of the car. We were at the border in less than two hours. It wouldn't be until after the revolutions of 1989 that we'd learn how mad a coincidence it had been, and how very badly it should have gone:

Strolling down memory lane, my father had found the one spot offering a perfect visual overview of one of the top-secret Soviet missile sites in Czechoslovakia.

Idiocy has its privileges, my mother maintained. As does truth, apparently: Our story of cows and camping had been too unbelievable *not* to be true—no actors in the world could have cooked that up on the fly. For whatever reason—though I doubt he was a man given to sentiment—our friend delayed reporting us long enough for us to make the border.

He'd have a story to tell his wife that evening.

LI

WE RETURNED HOME AND the world shut down. The humor faded, the fights grew worse. It wasn't all one thing or the other; there were bouts of normalness, of joy throughout. The better times would still show up, like old friends who can't stand to see you fall, for years to come.

During the decades of Soviet occupation, the Czechs developed a fine catalog of jokes at the Russians' expense—the power of the powerless, truly. On any given bus ride, some drunk brave with slivovitce would stand and deliver, swaying lightly, for the pleasure of all concerned: "You know the one about . . . ?"

"Did you hear? The Americans have developed a new kind of submarine. It winds through the water like this, like a snake, to avoid the mines."

"Yeah? Big deal. The Russians have a new submarine that goes like this—up and down, like a roller coaster."

"What's the point of that?"

"It lets the rowers catch a breath."

My mother was that Russian submarine. For a long time she rose and fell, caught her breath, then submerged again. It wasn't one thing or the other. It was never one thing or the other. It would have been easier if it had. Eventually the trips to the surface came less frequently. Until they stopped altogether.

Was she bipolar? Very possibly. Was it the benzodiazepines? They didn't help. Was it the toxin of incest, the loneliness of exile? Was it depression, her marriage to my father, her nature?

Most things in life are multiple-choice questions. There is no answer key.

Which never stopped me from wondering. Or from standing back in dumb amazement at the turns that even the most damaged life can take—the power that a drowning soul can summon.

"Do not go gentle into that good night?" When it came to Mom, going gentle was never a risk.

The year after our close call, we spent the summer at Twin Lakes. The descent had begun in earnest. Two years later we moved to Bethlehem and the pull of the bottom grew stronger. The thing with girls had begun; the crazy, screaming, staggering-down-the-hall rages, the days and weeks of depression. She began to hallucinate, claiming she'd gone to New York, that she'd seen an old woman with periwinkle-blue eyes lying on the floor at the Port Authority. That she'd tried to help her, then left to get her some food only to find her dead on her return. That the police officer she alerted to the dead woman by the wall had sneered, "Yeah, so what? There's plenty of dead people in New York."

My mother hadn't been to New York in weeks, and one of the things she was most vain about were her "periwinkle-blue eyes."

And then it happened.

I should have predicted it—it had happened before. In 1946, sinking fast, she'd clawed her way to the surface—applied for a job teaching English in a language camp, packed a bag, walked down the platform, climbed on the train.

Twenty-eight years later she did it again, reversed the plunge. She applied for a visa, booked a ticket, called a cab to take her to Bethlehem's ABE airport. It was the summer of 1974. She was going home.

LII

IT WAS SURPRISINGLY EASY. She was allowed to stay. To rent an apartment. To teach English at various language camps in the summer. The Communist Party bureaucrats on Leninová ulice (Lenin Street) in Brno, where all foreigners had to report within forty-eight hours of entering the country, would ask the usual questions, listen attentively to her answers, mention in passing the appeal of digital watches or pocket calculators (my mother would take note for the future), then stamp what needed stamping. She would have to check in with the authorities on a regular basis. Changes in domicile would have to be reported immediately. But she had her three months.

In early summer, with the linden trees newly leafed out and everything—the dust, the stone, the herbs in the gardens—smelling just the way they had, it must have seemed as if time had stopped and only the people continued on, aging in a frozen world. Uncle Pepa and Aunt Sonya were still in the house they'd always been in. Her friend Jiřinka was unchanged—the same steady soul, the same quiet laugh—just the hair, the eyes, a slight heaviness in the step.

Her father was still living in the same house she'd grown up in on Zeyrová Street, remarried now. She'd last seen him in the early sixties when he'd visited us in the old apartment in Queens in the dead of winter. She paid a call one afternoon, met her stepmother. The three of them shared little sandwiches—*chlebíčky*—drank some coffee, and then her father stood up and she left. He seemed neither interested nor uninterested in her. He'd been doing fine without her.

She learned the rules of life under the new regime, adapted well, mastered the fine art of bribery like no one else. Rummaging through her purse at Leninová ulice, playing the scatterbrained, flustered woman to perfection, she'd spill out her compact, her sunglasses, her makeup, a pocket calculator, then wait for the inevitable compliment and push it over (barely noticing, still rummaging), with a casual "Please, take it, I have another," sail through the obligatory protestations—he couldn't possibly—then cut them off at just the right moment: Ah, *here* it was—the paper she'd been looking for. The calculator had vanished. Everything was understood. Welcome home, Pani Sloukova.

Of course, what was a game to her—and to me, later, for she taught me well—was less amusing to everyone else. Corrupted from inside, the regime stood like a rickety house, teetering on collapse; collaborators were everywhere, as were those who hated them and yearned for the day when the tables would turn—people who labored under menial jobs, who couldn't speak or think aloud, whose children were denied entrance to the university because of their parents' refusal to join the Party. To her credit, my mother never forgot this, and did what little she could—tactfully taking care of the bills, quietly tanking up the car while her friends were in the restaurant, making it easy.

She was forty-nine that summer. Still beautiful, I think. I visited her there that first July. She showed me all the places she'd known as a girl, introduced me to Jiřinka, who I liked immediately, brought me to meet my great-aunt and -uncle, who took me in, told me stories, fed me. I hadn't seen my mother so happy in a long time. Like someone condemned to be shot at dawn, then reprieved at the last moment, she was learning to believe again. She and Jiřinka would drive into the country, stopping here or there, at this restaurant or that one, picking mushrooms or swimming in ponds, then make their way back to Brno with the wind drying their hair, sunburned and singing.

In the summer of 1975, my mother and Jiřinka took a long weekend and drove out to the Vysočina highlands—there was a little restaurant Jiřinka had heard about, the forests were beautiful and endless, and the week's rain would mean mushrooms.

The restaurant was only so-so but the woods were lovely, the water cool and refreshing, and they lay on their stomachs in the high grass and talked like they used to when they were fifteen, then meandered back to the car, where they changed out of their bathing suits. They'd try to get a room in a little hotel they knew in Račín, they'd decided—stretch things out another day.

It was one of those afternoons in June—strong sun, dark

shadows—with dustings of blossoms on the roads and just enough breeze to make the clothes feel good on your body. At a crowded intersection in Žďár my mother hesitated (she'd always been a timid driver), missed her turn to go, then hesitated again. Cars began to honk. Flustered, still learning to drive stick, hemmed in by male drivers whose cheap Trabants ran on an Italianate mixture of testosterone and impatience—my mother stalled out. Increasingly frantic, she restarted the engine, let up on the clutch, started to move . . . and stopped.

Halfway into the intersection now, she put the car in neutral, then turned off the engine. Jiřinka, who had the unflappable cool of a nineteenth-century schoolteacher or an RAF fighter pilot, asked her what she was doing. My mother, as if hypnotized, opened her door and stepped out of the car.

Across the intersection, like a boulder in a river of swerving automobiles, another car had come to a stop. Its door was open. A man in a white summer shirt and dark slacks was standing next to it.

It was the most extraordinary thing she'd ever seen, Jiřinka said. They were looking at each other across that intersection as if they couldn't hear the chaos around them—as if nothing else in the world existed.

LIII

AND REALITY OUTRAN THE dream. As it sometimes will.

Can I explain how they recognized each other behind the windshields of their cars across a gap of fifty feet and twenty-seven years? No, I can't. It seems impossible, and when you consider that most of us only see what we anticipate seeing anyway, as if our expectations prepared the world for our coming, it seems even more impossible. And yet I believe it. I don't have a choice. Jiřinka could no more embellish a story than I could sing opera.

In truth, how it happened doesn't matter. It happened. The end validated the means. Except it wasn't the end. It was a beginning.

It would be nice to think that those touched by more than their share of grief come in for a refund; that the Fates, acknowledging that they've piled on, throw us a tidbit: "Here, take it, it's yours—a little something for all you've lost."

In my mother's case they did exactly that. In fact, they out-did themselves, engineering something so unlikely, so much like fiction, that if you found it in a novel you'd put the book aside in favor of something closer to life. But I didn't read it in a novel. I saw it. This was the great compensation of my mother's life—the not-quite-saving grace. And the force of it swept disbelief from its path like dust.

Everything began again exactly where it had left off. Effortlessly. As if they'd seen each other the weekend before. As if Innsbruck and Naples and Australia, that dank and beautiful house outside Munich and the Manhattan skyline rising out of the fog, hadn't happened yet—or had been a memory all along.

I've never been able to laugh at love, though it's tempting. We're so dazed, so vulnerable—dropping things, not hearing things, then smiling, almost wistfully, like people caught remembering something long ago—so obviously in a state of grace that we can't *help* being a target. And maybe it's because we're so easy to take down in those moments, and because we don't care if we are, that I've never joined in. It seemed unsporting; better to stand back, watch it run.

I suppose I could have hated my mother for her love affair with F., seen it as a betrayal of my father, used it against her for all the grief she'd given me for my own loves. I never did. I wasn't being noble; it just never occurred to me. It seemed like a miracle, and I didn't believe in miracles.

The facts were straightforward. F. was unhappily married, with two grown sons. His wife was a decent woman, a good mother; he wouldn't talk against her—he certainly didn't blame her—but their marriage had been built on habit, not love. For a while it had seemed enough. There'd been affection between them once, but affection had passed into tolerance, silence—*I'm sorry, did you say something?*—mutual invisibility. They both knew this—had talked about separation for a decade or more; she wouldn't hear of it.

He'd never expected to see my mother again. Hardly even thought of their time together anymore. The years had come on and that was all right. He didn't mind so much. He'd been a boy when she left. He took pleasure in his sons, in his work; he had friends in Žďár he saw quite often. Whatever he'd once felt was like a fire in a closed room; he expected it would take the rest of his life to go out. It was all right.

And now, in one instant, the room had been thrown open, the windows and doors ripped off their hinges. They were standing at the intersection. It was all still there. And it blazed.

It lasted four, maybe five, summers—I can't be sure. I witnessed it, I was there—my mother's confidant, her co-conspirator. I aided and abetted and I can't find it wrong. I liked this man: the way he carried himself, the way he talked to me—neither condescending nor ingratiating but measured, listening. I liked the way my mother was in his company, the way he seemed by some magic to have returned her to herself. And to me. I'd been living with my parents' misery for years. I thought this could save them both.

And so for those four or five summers, my mother and F. did what people in love (who aren't supposed to be) have always done:

lied so they could be together. Making up stories of weeklong con-
ferences in Budapest or trips to Prague, they'd sneak off like teen-
agers to some shack in the woods where they'd cook their meals
on a single-burner Primus and lower the milk and the cheese into
a meter-deep hole under the floorboards to keep it cool. When it
rained they'd take long, dripping walks through the woods or pick
raspberries in the clear-cuts or drive out to some out-of-the-way
place for lunch, and when there was sun, they'd lie in the sun in the
grass by one of the lonely little ponds Moravia is known for until
it was time for him to go or until September had come, which was
when my mother would put down everything that sustained her
and return for the year to Bethlehem.

And then May would arrive, and in the halls of Freedom High
School the kids would be wearing cutoffs and Mom would be packing to leave for another summer. And when she arrived in Brno,
sometimes with her friends still laughing and eating pastries in the
living room, she'd sneak off and call F.'s office in Žďár—they had
a code to let him know she was in the country—and everything
would begin again. They were thinking of getting married, she
told me. Now that I was older it seemed that maybe . . . I had to tell
her the truth—did I like him?

Very much, I told her, pleased with how mature I sounded,
grateful that my opinion still mattered to her; grateful, as well, not
to be taking fire for being in love myself. After all, I said, we could
both admit that things with Dad had been difficult for years.

"I just want you both to be happy," I remember saying to her
once, and meaning it, while not unpleased with how well the halo
suited me. It was dusk, June, the air thick with the smell of cut

fields and still water. The evening's first coolness was coming off the fields. We were walking along the small dirt path that wound around Skalák, the same pond where, just a little ways further down the shore, she'd count out for me the number of pills it would take to stop her life.

LIV

I'M SUSPICIOUS OF MEMORY, though I've played in its fields all my life. I don't trust how it accommodates us, how it adjusts to whatever it thinks we want, smiles or snarls as we do. Sometimes I think it's just a mirror of our moods, a step away from mimicry.

A strange thought: The past lightens, darkens, lightens again—like a landscape under passing clouds—because somewhere in the future, years ahead, someone just had an argument with their boss.

I want to believe that those four or five summers my mother and F. were together in the 1970s were blissful, stolen seasons. That they were a compensation for all the pain behind her and all the pain to come. I want to believe that very much. It would make things easier—for me, mostly.

Alas, wanting to believe ain't enough. You have to check yourself, learn to spot the seductive shape of narrative, which bends things to its will. As the Czechs like to say of their dealings with the Russians, *Dověřuj, ale provjeřuj*—Trust, but verify.

The summers my mother spent with F. in the 1970s were some of the happiest times of her life—I'm as sure of this as I am of anything on earth—*and* they were larded with pain. With him she soared—repaired, reborn. Away from him, she plunged. For me.

It's interesting to think how much damage people do, to others as well as to themselves, out of a sense of obligation. "I'm doing this for you," they say, "because it's the right thing to do, because I love you," yet give it a little time—wait for a moment of weakness or anger—and the real words rise to the surface: "I'm suffering for you, because I love you—and the least you can do is be grateful."

I wasn't the only reason my mother had to return to Bethlehem, but I was the main one and I knew it. Every September she'd come home to Lord Byron Drive, unpack, and the world would start to darken—because of me. And maybe it's because I still carry the crimeless guilt for those winters—it would have been kinder to us both if she'd stayed in Czechoslovakia—that I try not to inflict my righteousness on others, to do the martyr's dance. I have other failings. I owe her that.

But again, the darkness of Bethlehem was hardly total. There'd be times that were better—an hour here, an afternoon there. Music helped. We'd sit in the windowless dining room where the turntable was, and I'd play her records I thought she'd like: "Sweet Baby James" and "Bridge over Troubled Water" and singles from the tattered stack I kept in my room (singles I still listen to with our daughter), and even, once—I was feeling bold—some Creedence, which to my surprise she liked. "Who'll Stop the Rain?" was a wonderful song, she said.

It wasn't much and it didn't last. The music ended, the silence returned; the things hemming her in asserted themselves. A cartoon she clipped from the *Bethlehem Globe-Times*—which she kept for thirty-five years, and which I found in the papers in her house in Vydří—captured the view from her world: It shows a man, bleary with sleep, who's just gotten out of bed in his pajamas. It's the start of a new day. Ahead of him is a maze that stretches to the horizon.

The winters were endless. And they weren't. Time would go on—with or without her. Every March, obeying the call, the snow would obediently pull back against the walls and the fences. The diorama would fire, the lights would go on, and the figure frozen in the chair would take a sip from her cup. May would come.

Few things are as hard to capture as happiness that's passed. Especially someone else's. You're looking back, remembering what it was like. And there's nothing there. It's all moments, hints—discrete, mute—like tiny bits of film that have to be glued together to create the feeling, the time, or at least the illusion of it. Then again, sometimes a single piece can stand for the whole. I've saved one, like a piece of celluloid in an envelope.

I'd been staying in a little shack in the forests a long day's walk from the town of Telč. For a while there'd been a girl, but she'd returned to her family in Vyškov for a while, and I'd been spending the days alone, swimming in the ponds, thinking of her, walking to the village for supplies. A blissful time. The cabin had two wooden bunks, a hole under the floorboards that served as a refrigerator, a kerosene lamp for light.

When my mother came by, we sat on a mossy bench against the north wall and she told me that F. might be able to get away that night and I offered to clear out. I'd go camping, I said. She tried to argue with me—she didn't want to feel like she was pushing her own son into the woods—but I wouldn't hear it. It wasn't a big deal. It was summer. I'd be back the next day.

I remember that afternoon as one of the most beautiful I've known, though I couldn't tell you why. Beauty, like happiness, slips the sieve. Maybe there was something about the light, the big piled clouds to the west lending everything a clarity you could almost touch: the decaying stump hedged in ferns, the pool of shadow under pines, the midges dancing in a ray of light—all these seemed painted.

I hid my things in a thicket of brambles and spent the day wandering; I swam, read, then fell asleep in the grass. Waking up sun-stunned and stiff, I splashed some water on my face and started back toward the old logging road, a kilometer or two away, that had brought me there. It was getting late, and I had a good two-hour walk back to my things.

I remember that walk: the white-edged clouds in the darkening sky, the lupines along the ditch, the rows of lindens that marked the road's progress through the fields. In the forests it was always quiet, the tired sound of the insects far off, like a conversation in a distant room.

I'd gone around a bend in the road when I saw them and stopped. They were maybe a hundred yards ahead, walking through a tunnel of trees toward the light. The late sun was slanting across the field ahead of them, picking out the blood-spots of poppies in the grain. They had their arms around each other's waists, and as I watched, my mother lay her head on his shoulder.

And I remember something seizing me by the throat and having to blink my eyes to see, and then the road turned into the field and they disappeared behind the trees.

It rained that night. The old tent I'd found in the shack had no fly or groundcloth, and I woke up soaked, a small stream running under my shoulder blades. A storm came, then another. I tried to dig a trench in the dark with my hands but the soil was full of roots, and when I tried to push the earth up into a ridge, the pine-needly dirt crumbled in the rain.

At some point, knowing I couldn't return to the shack, I gathered my soaking things and made my way back to the place in the woods, maybe a quarter-mile away, where my mother had parked her car. It was locked, as I knew it would be, but it didn't matter. Crawling beneath the undercarriage, I dragged my things in after me and, unbelievably, fell asleep. I was eighteen. It didn't matter.

It was just after dawn when I woke to the sound of another car's motor, and looking out from between the front wheels, saw F.'s blue Škoda bump by in the fog. It stopped at the road, then turned right.

To the best of my recollection, I never saw him again.

LV

SOMETIME IN THE LATE spring of 1978 my mother returned to the apartment in Brno that she rented every summer. I was with her. Jiřinka and her friend Jucina were already there, waiting for us with cakes and wine, as were three or four other people I can't remember.

Strange that I can recall the cakes and wine but not how we got there. Had we flown into Vienna, then taken a bus? Had we rented a car?

We put our suitcases in the back bedroom. We could hear everyone laughing, pouring out the wine and talking over each other. I should go out, my mother said. She'd be right there. She'd bring the presents. And she smiled at me, because I knew she couldn't wait to call, and she knew that I knew it, and I smiled back. We'd always been friends. And I went to join the others.

My mother came into the living room a few minutes later carrying the half-dozen or so small presents we always brought with us—I vaguely remember a blue silk scarf and a bottle of Bailey's, though my mind may simply be filling in gaps, imagining—and then we spent the next few hours the way we often did there: eating, drinking, gossiping, talking about whatever it is that friends talk about. I vacuumed up enough pastries to make a small, sweet child. Jiřinka said it should be against the law to be able to eat like that and not be fat, and I answered her with my mouth full of custard and everybody laughed and complained about the injustice of it and how it would all catch up with me, I'd see, that I'd wake up one morning—maybe tomorrow—so fat I couldn't roll over, and I smiled and belched. Plans were made for the next day, and for the next weekend, and for the next three months.

Knowledge doesn't always change what you remember.

I remember it as a lovely, unremarkable afternoon. Even now.

Hours before our friends left, before she brought the presents from our suitcases into the living room, my mother made her call. They had a code of some kind. My mother, let's say, would call F.'s office claiming to be Alena Nováková, from firm such and such, and ask to speak to Engineer F.S. And F., hearing the code names, knowing my mother was back in the country, would tell his secretary he was busy, and that evening—that same hour, if he was able to escape—he'd call her back from a public phone.

And so my mother, sitting on the bed because of the short phone cord, called the number she kept all year in the envelope taped to the back of the dresser drawer. She was Alena Nováková, calling from firm X. Was engineer F.S. available?

There was a pause on the line that she put down to a bad connection.

"I'm sorry," said the woman, her voice altered, "are you a friend of Engineer S.?"

"I am," my mother said, feeling her world gathering into a drop.

"Then I'm terribly sorry to have to tell you that Engineer S. passed away last week—a sudden heart attack, I'm afraid."

And the drop fell. My mother hung up the phone.

But even this would not be enough. Still in that shadow between hearing and understanding, my mother tried to save something. There would be letters. Her letters. She had to get them—she had to try to save the family the scandal. If she could get an appointment, talk her way into his office, maybe . . .

She called back. A different woman—younger, sounding rushed—answered the phone. My mother began to explain something about Engineer F.S.

"One moment, I'll connect you," the woman said.

And for those few seconds the world pulled back into shape, reconstituted itself—it was a mistake, she'd imagined it all—and then fate in its cruelty played its last card. A man answered the phone: a voice exactly like F.'s but thirty years younger, and she recalled hearing about the older son—an engineer like his father, his namesake—being hired the previous year.

Ano, mužu Vám s něčím pomoct? Yes, can I help you with something?

He had no idea she'd existed. He never would. He sounded like his father had in 1946.

Je někdo tam? Is someone there?

And I imagine my mother held on to that voice for a moment, then two, and then maybe one more, before laying the phone in its receiver.

Being my mother, she sat very quietly on the edge of the bed for a few seconds, then opened the suitcases, collected the presents, and walked toward our voices in the living room.

I wouldn't learn till later that night that he was gone.

And I think it's only now, looking out at the pasture wall running down into the lake, that I see that that afternoon I lost her, too.

LVI

YOU WONDER ABOUT THINGS. I've wondered for years why she didn't say anything that afternoon, what compelled her to come out of that bedroom, knowing that her life was basically over, and put on that act. It never made sense to me: Most of the people in that room knew about F. already, and the others surely wouldn't have suspected anything to see her upset because a close friend of hers had died unexpectedly. Why would she ask that of herself? Why would she make herself endure something so useless?

For a while, groping for an answer, I put it down to her over-blown sense of social propriety, her stiff-upper-lipness, her admiration for Somerset Maugham's colonials, insisting on getting dressed for tea in some malarial jungle: "Yes, but one must do what one must, musn't one," etc. It never quite fit.

Revelations stutter into view—in dreams, through words, some more welcome than others. And though I distrust revelation—it smacks of impatience, the desire to be done, the hurried nail in the coffin—this one might stand: My mother did what she did because, over the years, pain had become personified, plural—a *them* to be resisted, to be denied their pleasure. But this wasn't like Ahab, projecting the world's pain (and his own) on something outside of himself and then, "as though his chest were a mortar, wreaking his hot, heart's shell upon it"; this was something closer to Kafka. *They*, the ones responsible, the sources of all pain, were inside you. The ultimate battleground—which would swallow both sides—was the self.

I have a photograph of my mother that I don't look at very often. Almost never, actually. There's no date, but it's from the seventies because she's maybe forty-five or fifty. Still young, still beautiful. It's summer somewhere in Czechoslovakia, and she's wearing a bathing suit, lying on a towel in the grass. She's smiling up at the camera. Her father, in a track suit, is lying next to her.

How it came to be I have no idea. The usual way, I imagine. She'd be invited to their cottage; there'd be a picnic. And she'd go because she had to, because *they* had to be resisted. And when someone with a camera suggested a father and daughter picture, she smiled, and meant it, because *they* would be denied their pleasure. Because *they* would never see her pain.

How quickly I'd save her now—from them, from herself. Assuming she'd let me, which I doubt. Because at some point, *they*—the ones who wished her harm, who were cruel, unjust—grew to include me.

I have a vague memory of us being invited to my grandfather's *chata* in the country, though I don't know where it was or when, what we could have talked about or why we went.

For all I know, I could have taken the picture. And I'm haunted by it. That she's smiling at me, pleading with me, asking me to read her. And I can't.

LVII

THE REST WAS WHAT it was—not a happy ending. My mother-in-law, who can't abide unhappy endings, probably wouldn't like it. My mother returned to Bethlehem, because it didn't matter. I'd come home from college once a month to find a quarter-inch of dust on the record we'd listened to the last time I was there.

The vortex strengthened—the craziness, the delusions, the rages grew worse. My parents separated, then divorced—by now my father's place among the enemies, like my own, was official. When the Velvet Revolution of 1989 returned Czechoslovakia to itself, they both returned home, my father to Prague and, eventually, a new marriage; my mother to Vydří. At one point, after she and the man she lived with kicked us out of their home with our eighteen-month-old daughter and four-year-old son (after refusing to let us borrow the car to buy diapers, then screaming at us to hose off the rash-covered toddler in the yard), I didn't talk to her for seven years. I didn't miss it. I'd dream about her now and then, let whatever pain or regret I felt seep down into an aquifer I hoped was limitless, and go my way. I didn't miss it.

And if, in some sense, it didn't matter—if it was actually done the afternoon she heard a voice on the other end of the phone saying "Then I'm very sorry to have to tell you . . . ," if she basically walked under a bus the next year while still living in Bethlehem— the life remaining still had to be dealt with.

She wouldn't go easy—not my mother. She'd build her nightmares in the air, then put foundations under them. My father would save himself, barely; find some measure of peace, come to love our children. I'd anchor myself like a tent in the wind to my own family. My mother, meanwhile, would return to Czechoslovakia alone—confirming the Gypsy's prophesy—scorning all help, raging at the world.

There'd be collateral damage. But in her fury, battling to the last vestige of memory, she'd make herself into a kind of art.

Am I being clever at my mother's expense? Trust me, no.

It came to me in Vydří last summer. There, within arm's reach of her bed in that boarded-up, piled bedroom, were the letters, the quietly moldering journals, the curling pictures of F. as a young man, of me as a child, of the grandchildren she'd never wanted to know. It seemed extraordinary to me—the way she'd cocooned herself in heartache, surrounding herself with precisely those things calibrated to hurt her most. There was a kind of genius to it.

It was a talent I recognized. This was my inheritance, a gift I'd spent half a century hemming in with happiness. But if my own talent for regret was notable—worth a polite round of applause, no more—hers was thunderous, undeniable, damn near demonic.

Nobody could mourn the past like she could. She was the Mozart of pain, playing herself to the end.

Three days after our trip to Vydří, sitting on a bench in a forgotten little park in Prague that I love, it occurred to me that it was a shame that my mother and Kafka, who died the year before she was born, had missed each other. He would have liked her. Understood her. In some ways he'd imagined her—her inner exile, her guilt, her lust for atonement. Her ability to punish herself so exquisitely.

In "In the Penal Colony," Kafka's *Meisterstück* of cruelty and existential guilt, a torture instrument inscribes the prisoner's crime—whatever commandment he's said to have disobeyed—deeper and deeper into his skin. The condemned is strapped naked to a mechanism called the "bed," which "quivers in minute, very rapid vibrations" corresponding very exactly to "the harrow" above it—an instrument consisting of harrow-like needles. The condemned has no opportunity to defend himself because "guilt is not to be doubted." Nor will he (or she) be told his sentence because, given time—and the harrow takes a long time to complete its work—he will "learn it on his body."

In her last years—and I'd have torn them off this story the way Marlow tears the end off Kurtz's letter in *Heart of Darkness* if I didn't know she'd despise me for it—my mother at long last turned the harrow on herself. Year after year she executed the sentence and endured it, inscribing into her skin, deeper and deeper, the names of the things she'd loved and lost—creating a self-portrait of unendurable pain and unbendable endurance in perfect equipoise, like two wrestlers matched to the last atom until—and here was the turn to genius only Kafka could have imagined—when the man she'd loved left her for good, when the past she mourned became familiar and dull, she invented losses that had never occurred, like the loss of my love, and mourned those.

I don't know that she had a choice. And all I can be is sorry for it. And let her go.

LVIII

I DON'T BELIEVE IN beginnings. Or endings. I just don't.

She died yesterday. An e-mail from Brno. Sitting here, the room lightens, then darkens. A pattering of warm rain, then sun. I can smell the garden.

We're a run-on sentence. All of us, every last mother's son.

LIX

It's morning, early. The house at Twin Lakes is quiet, the air coming in the window, cool and sweet.

I'll sneak out the back, jump on my bicycle. I'll pick her some flowers. It'll make her happy.

Acknowledgments

I'm so grateful to have so many to be grateful to.

First, this book wouldn't exist if my wife, Leslie, hadn't understood that the time had come for me to write it. And said so. If our kids, Maya and Zack, hadn't backed her up, pushed me through, and, like Leslie, read and re-read. So here it is, guys. Without your love, I wouldn't have had the courage. Then again, without your love, it wouldn't matter.

I want to thank a handful of trusted friends for their early readings: Richard Abramowitz, Beth Beringer, Geoff Chin, Brian Hall, Dan Raeburn, Victoria Redel.

I'm indebted to my editor, Jill Bialosky, for her early encouragement, her steady support, and, not least, for suggesting the title for *The New Yorker* essay that became the title of this book. I'm grateful to her and to the folks at Norton for giving this orphan a home that *feels* like a home.

Finally, I owe a growing debt to my agent, Bill Clegg, whose instincts I've come to trust implicitly, whose diagnoses are as accurate as his bedside manner is frank, supportive, generous. What more could you want?